U:P:D:A|||||||||||||||||E

New directions in geographical fieldwork

David Job

CAMBRIDGE
UNIVERSITY PRESS

QUEEN MARY
AND WESTFIELD COLLEGE
UNIVERSITY OF LONDON

PUBLISHED BY THE PRESS SYNDICATE OF THE UNIVERSITY OF CAMBRIDGE
The Pitt Building, Trumpington Street, Cambridge CB2 1RP, United Kingdom

CAMBRIDGE UNIVERSITY PRESS
The Edinburgh Building, Cambridge CB2 2RU, UK   www.cup.cam.ac.uk
40 West 20th Street, New York, NY 10011-4211, USA   www.cup.org
10 Stamford Road, Oakleigh, Melbourne 3166, Australia
Ruiz de Alarcón 13, 28014 Madrid, Spain

First published 1999

Printed in Great Britain at the University Press, Cambridge

Typeface *Times*   System *Pagemaker 6.5*®

A catalogue record for this book is available from the British Library

ISBN 0 521 46845 0 paperback

Cover picture, showing a group of students engaged in fieldwork, is by David Job

Update

Update is produced from the Department of Geography at Queen Mary and Westfield College (QMW), University of London, by an editorial board with expertise from across the fields of Geography and Education. The editor is Geraldene Wharton. *Update* is a unique project in educational publishing. It is aimed at A-level students and first-year undergraduates in geography. The objective of the series, which ranges across both physical and human geography, is to combine the study of major issues in the geography syllabus with accounts of especially significant case studies. Each *Update* incorporates a large amount of empirical material presented in easy-to-read tables, maps and diagrams. We hope that you find the series as exciting to use as we find it to produce. The editor would be delighted to receive any suggestions for further *Update*s or comments on how we could make the series even more useful.

The author

David Job worked for the Field Studies Council for many years, most recently at Slapton Ley Field Centre, teaching and developing field courses in A-level geography. After a period of school teaching he joined the Geography Education section at the Institute of Education, University of London where he developed the Earth Science Process Centre and co-ordinated a school-based project investigating air pollution. He then set up the Ecological Education Partnership at Magdalen Farm, Dorset with Gyles Morris, a project integrating geographical fieldwork with organic farming and sustainability issues.

Acknowledgements

Many of the ideas developed in this volume owe a great deal to discussion and debate with several former colleagues, friends, researchers, and visiting teachers and students with whom I worked while at Slapton Ley Field Centre. The stimulating and convivial company and the thoughts and ideas of Gyles Morris, Nigel Coles, Keith Chell, Sarah-Jane Burr and Richard Irvine deserve special mention. Research undertaken by Phil Harvey at Slapton while at Durham University provided the crucial springboard for exploring more qualitative approaches to fieldwork. The support and critique of former colleagues at the Institute of Education, notably Frances Slater, David Lambert and Ashley Kent, is very much appreciated. I owe thanks to the editorial board of the *Update* series, Mike McPartland and David Caton and his students for valued criticism of the text. Henrietta Pomroy sustained and encouraged me with merriment, flowers and cups of tea when other projects threatened to prevent completion of the book.

Contents

Glossary

The following explanations of possibly unfamiliar terminology in the text are not dictionary definitions but are based upon the geographical context in which they are used in this book.

Acclimatisation: Engaging in experiences which enable one to become more familiar with and accustomed to an unfamiliar environment.

Anthropocentric: Describes a viewpoint which values nature and resources primarily in terms of their usefulness to humans.

Attitudes: Opinions about specific issues which arise from and are informed by values.

Chaos theory: The theory that small variations in conditions can become amplified to produce large and often unpredictable outcomes.

Direct action: Acting individually or with others to challenge and resist change or practices to which one is opposed.

Ecocentric: Describes a view of the Earth and nature which gives equal value to all life forms, values spiritual as well as scientific understandings of the Earth, and encourages forms of human activity which minimise their impact on natural systems and processes.

Environmental determinism: A somewhat discredited approach in geography which regards the human landscape and culture as determined simply by physical factors.

Feedback: Where one factor has an effect on another in a system, a change in the first factor alters a second factor which then produces further changes which feed back to alter the first factor. Positive feedback occurs if an increase (or decrease) in the initial factor results in an intensified increase (or decrease) in that factor, i.e. a snowballing effect. Negative feedback occurs when a change in the initial factor is brought in check by the feedback process and the system is self-limiting.

Gaia hypothesis: An interpretation of the Earth put forward by James Lovelock proposing that the Earth functions in a similar way to a living organism, regulating itself to changing conditions in ways that enable life (in its broadest sense) to be sustained.

Holistic: Defines broad views of environments which concentrate on whole systems and the interconnections and relationships between the parts.

Hypothesis: A proposition or explanation yet to be supported by objective evidence.

Idiographic: Describes explanations applicable only to the immediate local circumstances which are not widely applicable to a wide variety of situations (*see* Nomothetic).

Modernism: The dominant world view of the Western world over the past four centuries in which phenomena and events are interpreted on the basis of objective knowledge, classical science and linear sequences of cause and effect.

Nomothetic: Describes explanations of phenomena based on widely applicable and generalised laws (*see* Idiographic).

Palimpsest: The superimposition of 'layers' of human imprint on a landscape over historic time whereby each additional culture only partially obscures the features from previous cultures.

Postmodernism: An emerging way of interpreting phenomena and events which denies objective knowledge, accepting that every explanation is affected by individual experience and cultural perspective, thus rejecting absolute certainties about anything.

Reductionism: A belief that an understanding of a large or complex system can be achieved by studying the functioning of its individual components or subsystems.

Sense of place: Having deep feelings for the character of a place and thereby valuing its distinctiveness.

Sensory: Describes responses to an environment or experience which affect the senses and emotions.

Sustainability/Sustainable development: Ways of living, producing things and social organisation which can be maintained over long periods of time without depleting resources, causing pollution or exploiting nature, other people or cultures.

Technocentric: Defines a view which considers that the natural world can be controlled to meet human needs through the use of technology and scientific knowledge. Environmental problems can be solved through technical intervention without having to fundamentally alter human activity.

Values: The deeply-held beliefs of an individual, society or culture about fundamental concerns such as priorities in life, justice, views of nature, beauty etc. which inform and give rise to more specific attitudes.

1 Introduction

Fieldwork – measurement or feeling?

On the geography shelves of your library you will probably find several books on fieldwork which offer ideas for fieldwork projects, techniques for collecting data in different environments and methods for analysing your findings and presenting and interpreting the results. This one is a little different in that it is not primarily a collection of techniques, though it does include some field methods which may be new to you.

It takes as a starting point some reactions to the sort of fieldwork that emphasises techniques for the collection of data. Here are two such responses, one from a teacher, the other from an A-level student:

> *The whole repertoire of fieldwork techniques was focused on this tiny village – yet its essence remained hidden . . . The feelings we had experienced during our visits could not be quantified or analysed. We were falling into the trap of classifying too much and enjoying too little.*
> (Brough, 1983)

> *I found myself getting really annoyed about what had been done to this village. I'm not sure that geographers are supposed to get worked up. They're just supposed to analyse. But this was the reason I got enthusiastic about what we were doing . . .*
> (quoted in Harvey, 1991)

These two reflections suggest that the data collection approach to fieldwork may be at odds with some of the more spontaneous ways in which we respond to places. Both experiences involved work in villages, though they could equally have been studies of rivers, cities, coasts or ecosystems. The first quotation is from a geography teacher who after undertaking exhaustive (and possibly exhausting) quantitative fieldwork methods with his pupils, felt that there was something missing from the experience. The techniques-oriented approach which had been adopted did not seem to have fulfilled one of the purposes traditionally associated with geography fieldwork, namely the development of a sense of place, that somewhat elusive feeling of every place having its own personality and character arising from the unique coming together of rocks, landscape, culture and climate. We might go further in our criticism and suggest that by not valuing and nurturing a sense of place through our experiences in the field, we have unwittingly contributed to a growing and creeping sense of placelessness.

It is some time now since geographers developed an enthusiasm for measurement and data collection in the field, often as a means of testing models or hypotheses against real world situations. The priority at the time was to arrive at generally applicable statements about patterns and processes in the landscape, even perhaps to establish geographical laws comparable to scientific laws. At the height of this trend in geography, some human geographers commented that in keeping with their search for generality, the world was becoming progressively more uniform and human activities seemed to be increasingly independent of physical influences:

> *. . . everywhere in the world is rapidly becoming more and more like everywhere else, and man's activities and pattern of life are becoming progressively divorced from the immediate physical conditions.*
> (Chorley, 1970)

Such a view is countered by more recent thoughts from geographers. Andrew Goudie, in considering the present state of physical geography, recognises the enduring relevance of physical factors in producing richness and diversity in the landscape: 'The whole world is not like Swindon and will never become so' (Goudie, 1994). His optimism though, in terms of the human impact on landscape, may only be valid if we learn to value the 'specialness' of different places through our fieldwork.

In the second quotation at the start of this introduction, a student felt angry while carrying out fieldwork in a village which she felt had been spoiled by inappropriate development. This emotional response seems to have happened despite, rather than because of, the data collection she was undertaking, though the instructions to map and count had provided her with a reason for being there. It is perhaps a little worrying that the view of geography which she had acquired was one which didn't allow feelings about places to be

Figure 1.1   Some perceptions of fieldwork.
Copyright (1999) United Feature Syndicate, Inc. Reproduced by permission

considered as somehow an appropriate part of a geographical experience. She seemed to have the idea that it was only the data which really mattered, not her feelings. We also get the impression that it was her emotional reaction to the place which generated her interest, rather than the coldly detached process of data collection and analysis.

Such reactions to fieldwork experiences are by no means unique. It is interesting to note some of the negative images of school field trips that occasionally appear in Peanuts cartoons (Figure 1.1)

As we will be exploring in later chapters, although fieldwork based on data collection and quantitative techniques is a worthwhile undertaking, both as a way of learning and as a way of increasing geographical understanding, an overemphasis on quantification may be limiting our natural inclinations to explore, interpret and draw meaning from the places we visit, in our own way.

One of the aims of this book is to consider some ways of going about fieldwork which could encourage us to express our feelings about places

as a valid part of geographical experience while incorporating the sort of investigation and enquiry which help us to increase our geographical understanding. An approach to fieldwork is offered which starts with our personal experience of places then, after a period of reflection, refines and feeds these experiences into more structured and comprehensive geographical enquiry.

Fieldwork and environmental priorities

The new directions for fieldwork outlined in this book are not only the result of critical reflections on some of the heavily quantitative approaches of recent years. They are also a response to changes taking place in the wider world. Such changes may have important implications not only for *what* we study through fieldwork but also *how* we go about it. An awareness of environmental degradation, resource depletion and social inequality has already led many fieldwork investigations to focus on issues which address or relate to these areas of concern. This should not detract from studies that do not focus directly on matters of environmental or social concern, though increasingly many areas of physical geography which we study in the field are influenced and altered to some degree by human activity. Similarly few aspects of the human landscape can be separated from issues of quality of life and social justice.

There are powerful arguments for enabling the priorities of the environmental agenda to inform our choices of what we study through fieldwork and where we carry out our investigations. Traditionally, physical geographers in particular have often gravitated to pleasant rural locations for their fieldwork and there are convincing reasons for continuing to do so. There may be a sound argument for retreating to places where naturalness and wildness still hold sway, to remind ourselves of the cyclical, conserving ways of nature which contrast so starkly with many of the linear resource pathways in cities which gobble resources at one end and churn out waste at the other.

However, should we not be directing our energies more specifically to those places that are most threatened, most degraded and most divided? Are the items on the environmental and social agenda too urgent to allow us to continue indulging ourselves in rural idylls on our field trips? Not that rural environments are devoid of important and relevant issues. In deciding priorities for the focus of fieldwork activities we may need to consider some difficult questions. Do the problems of urban air pollution and the condition of low-lying coasts and estuaries in a possibly warmer world have a greater priority at present over studies of hill slope shape or the orientation of glacial cirques in the Lake District? On the other hand, if we suggest that only those aspects of physical geography which relate to the human environment are worthy of study, are we not falling into the trap of undervaluing nature and landscape for their own sake, regardless of their 'usefulness' or relevance to human well-being?

Consideration of different environmental viewpoints may also be relevant to how we go about fieldwork and what we eventually do with our findings. We no longer have a single environmental viewpoint to inform our fieldwork. Some years ago, a field investigation with an environmental focus might well have concluded with recommendations for a neat technological fix – a sea wall perhaps to protect the threatened village, or raising river embankments to try and prevent flooding. More recent viewpoints about the Earth and our relationship with the natural world would be highly critical of such localised technical interventions. It would be argued that localised

cases of coastal erosion need to be viewed in the context of the whole sediment system of which that piece of coast is a part, while the urban flood problem should be related to processes and change in the whole catchment. Studies that place local problems and issues in a wider context are likely to come up with rather different recommendations than the local technical fix.

Studying wholes rather than parts is only one aspect of an emerging environmentalism which challenges technical 'solutions' to problems. Questions are now being asked as to whether we can really continue to regard the Earth as a huge machine whose mechanisms can be understood through scientific investigation and whose behaviour can be predicted and even controlled when things seem to be going wrong. In a recent book on different environmental viewpoints the author suggests that:

> *Nature is not only more complex than we presently know but also quite possibly more complex than we can know.*
> (Eckersley, 1992)

If this is true – and ideas from the Gaia hypothesis and chaos theory (see Chapter 2) suggest that it may be – then we need to treat our quantitative fieldwork data with some caution, realise its limitations and perhaps accept that there may be other pathways to understanding the Earth than through scientific investigation alone.

The relevance of these emerging world views to geography in general and fieldwork in particular require careful treatment. It is hoped that Chapter 2 will provide not only a background for the new fieldwork directions identified in later chapters (3–6) but will also serve as a summary of the new ways of viewing the Earth and our place in it and how these relate to geography more generally.

Investigation into action?

Despite the apparent relevance of many field-based investigations there is often a sense that many such investigations fail to follow through the implications of their findings. If we investigate urban air pollution and our findings show levels thought to be damaging to human health and the atmosphere, do we just write up the results, present it for assessment and file it away? Environmental abuses or social injustice are frequently identified in geographical projects, which are then put to one side and the potential of their findings to promote change for a better world is rarely realised. It is not perhaps surprising that few students who set out on an issue-based project actually follow through their findings and consider the relevance of these to their own lifestyles or seek to implement change and influence policy. There are few guidelines to facilitate this process. The final chapter of this book includes a range of options which might allow you to follow through findings from investigations into promoting change for a better world.

In summary then there are four aims to the new directions offered in this book:

- To consider the implications of changing viewpoints on how we go about fieldwork (Chapter 2).

- To review the range of fieldwork approaches adopted by geographers (Chapter 3).

- To seek ways of organising our fieldwork activities in order to recognise the value of both emotional responses to the places we visit and the geographical understanding to be gained from investigation and information gathering (Chapter 4).

- To offer examples of fieldwork in rural and urban environments which reflect new approaches and changing priorities (Chapters 5 and 6).

Listening

Sketching

Sensing

Figure 1.2   Students in the field.

Measuring

2 New world views: implications for fieldwork

- *Seeing local investigations in a wider context*

- *The relevance of environmental values to fieldwork*

- *Valuing what you feel as well as what you measure*

- *Fieldwork towards a better world*

Introduction

Towards the end of the 1960s many geographers adopted the statistical analysis of numerical data as the basis for their investigations. This change in method, away from descriptive approaches, came to be known as the quantitative revolution. Correspondingly, measurement and data collection became the most commonly practised style of geographical fieldwork. The new approach provided a structure and purpose to geographical investigation and gave the subject a scientific respectability which many geographers found reassuring. Furthermore, quantitative studies – that is, those involving measurement rather than just description – were regarded as contributing to an extension of our knowledge and understanding of the world.

This approach to fieldwork evolved at a time when there was considerable confidence in our ability to understand and make predictions about the behaviour of systems in physical geography, about the functioning and development of ecosystems and even social systems. Dividing the environment into subsystems was a convenient way of partitioning complex reality into manageable chunks. Understanding how the parts worked, it was thought, would lead to greater understanding of the whole. There were particular views about how systems responded to change, with a widely-held view that if systems (particularly natural systems) were disturbed they would tend to respond in ways which re-established balance, in other words they tended to adjust towards an equilibrium state. In considering interactions between the physical environment and human activity it was generally assumed that when problems such as pollution or resource scarcity arose, then new technology based on scientific research would provide solutions.

All of these previously assumed certainties are now being questioned. Recent thinking suggests that there is no longer a single accepted interpretation of anything – all interpretations spring from assumptions, and these vary according to the culture you come from, the society you live in and the values you hold. This is the essence of what has come to be known as *postmodernism*. In contrast, a *modernist* perspective was based on certainties, predictability, simple cause and effect and things being linked in a rather linear way, rather than more complex webs of interacting and possibly unpredictable factors (see Table 2.1).

The importance of such changes in thinking to geography and fieldwork are far-reaching. If we imagine going out on fieldwork in a group, for example, we could take the view that each individual has a different and personal response to a place. In a given place, we all have our own view of what is beautiful, ugly, important, interesting or dull. Deciding what is most worthwhile studying may need to take account of such individual perspectives. This is rather different from established approaches to fieldwork, perhaps involving hypothesis testing, or being taken on field excursions, where one person, the field leader or teacher, has decided from her or his viewpoint what is important in a landscape and therefore what we should be studying.

The following points summarise how some of the emerging new viewpoints may relate to how we go about fieldwork.

- Fieldwork investigations may need to focus on a small part of a larger system to be manageable but this approach may conflict with the emerging view that 'the whole is greater than the sum of its parts' (see sections in this chapter: 'Wholes and parts' and 'Here and there – local to global').

Table 2.1 Modernist and postmodernist views

	Modernist view	*Postmodernist view*
Ways of knowing	Only what is measurable is valid.	Information from our senses and feelings is as valid as quantifiable data.
View of nature	Nature exists as a resource for the convenience of and use by human beings.	Nature and landscape have a value and rights of their own regardless of their utilitarian value to humans.
Earth model	The functioning of the Earth can be understood by reducing the whole to its component parts. Scientific investigation of each part leads to an understanding of the whole.	The interactions amongst the Earth's subsystems are too complex and possibly unpredictable to be fully understood through scientific investigation alone.
Earth management	Harmful human impacts can be prevented or solved through management with appropriate technology.	Human activity should interfere as little as possible with other natural processes.

- If we are investigating people/environment issues then we need to recognise that there is a diversity of views about the relationship between people and the Earth. The old assumption that environmental problems could be solved by technical intervention is challenged by a number of other interpretations (see sections in this chapter: 'A robust or fragile Earth?', 'Nature- or people-centred views of the Earth?' and 'Fieldwork for a change – asking critical questions').

- If there are other ways of understanding and interpreting the Earth than those based exclusively on quantitative science, then we may be missing out on some important revelations if all we do in the field is count and measure. Some sorts of understanding may come to us via our senses, not exclusively through our powers of reasoning (see section in this chapter: 'Ways of knowing and understanding – science or senses?').

The following sections deal with a number of areas of debate where new viewpoints are challenging formerly established certainties. Each of these has important implications for the *what, why* and *how* of geographical fieldwork.

Wholes and parts

When undertaking a fieldwork investigation you will often be advised to focus your attention on a specific and local question, relationship or issue rather than making a broad or large-scale study. For example, you might be advised against studying the impact of London on global climate change and be directed more towards the effect of a small urban area on the local climate. This is sound practical advice in terms of producing a manageable investigation, but it is important to remember that though you may be looking at an apparently simple set of relationships at a local scale, perhaps only involving a few factors, there are probably many more variables which affect the system you are studying. The useful saying that 'the whole is greater than the sum of the parts' is a relevant idea to much of what we study in geography.

Many student fieldwork projects focus upon a hypothesis which examines the relationship between two or more factors. To make a study manageable and appropriate for the collection of quantitative data we often end up looking at small links in what is a much larger system with many links. If we only investigate a small link or relationship which forms a part of a larger system, we need to be aware that we are adopting what is sometimes called a *reductionist* point of view. Reductionism proposes that by studying each of the component parts of a larger system we can reach an overview of how the whole thing works. Thus, by studying the gearing, pedals, brakes and steering components of a bicycle we reach a reasonable understanding of how the whole machine works. This approach may work quite well for a relatively simple machine like a bicycle but there are doubts as to whether the same approach can be applied to the Earth with its interacting complex of physical, organic, social and political systems. For some time, the Western cultural perspective has tended to view the Earth as a giant machine whose behaviour can be understood, predicted and even controlled through careful investigation of the individual parts which make up the whole. Some more recent interpretations of the Earth rather question this view and suggest that reductionism may have some limitations.

The accumulation of knowledge about how small parts of the Earth system work and our limited understanding of how the whole thing operates have been likened to a building project where so much effort goes into making bricks that no-one gets round to putting them together to construct a building.

What significance do these changing interpretations of the Earth have on fieldwork in geography? Does it mean that our studies of small parts of larger systems are not worthwhile or valid? Clearly, we cannot hope to tackle all aspects of major environmental change in a school or college geography project. What we can do, though, is begin our study with a recognition of the broad picture, zoom in on something specific for our investigation, then return to the wider view to see how our focused study relates to the broader scene. The process might be likened to filming with a video camera where we might begin with a wide-angle shot, then zoom in on something of interest with the telephoto facility before returning to the wider view. Our review of the broader picture may well be different having examined some features in detail. Reductionism might be likened to filming many different features all in telephoto mode with no footage showing how individual details relate to each other and to the broader landscape.

The converse of reductionism is sometimes referred to as *holism*. The term 'holistic' is applied in many different contexts, not always appropriately, and has come to be a bit of a buzz word. You may have heard the term used in relation to alternative therapies in which health is considered with respect to the whole person, involving the physical body as well as mental and spiritual states. The approach differs rather from conventional medicine where physical symptoms are more likely to be related only to physical causes. Similarly, in the context of environmental concerns, changes and problems are viewed not just in terms of their immediate causes but related more widely to the social and political origins of changes that have an impact on the environment.

If our fieldwork is based on investigations of issues, reductionist viewpoints will tend to guide us towards simple but perhaps superficial solutions, while holistic approaches lead us more towards tackling the root causes of problems.

A robust or fragile Earth?

Lively debates continue among philosophers and scientists about how resilient the Earth may be to the impacts of human activity. Ecologists often refer to the fragility of particular ecosystems where a change in conditions might eliminate particular species or destroy a habitat. Whether the results of careless human impacts threaten life on Earth is less certain in the light of James Lovelock's Gaia hypothesis. Lovelock not only re-affirmed previous ideas about the interconnections between all parts of the Earth system but proposed the idea that the whole system had built-in devices which made it resilient to change rather than being fragile and vulnerable to destruction. Lovelock (1979) suggests that:

> *the earth's living matter, air, oceans and land surface form a complex system which can be seen as a single living organism which has the capacity to keep our planet a fit place for life.*

What may strike you initially about this statement is that several components of the Earth which we would not normally regard as 'living' are ascribed the attribute of life. Lovelock's ideas perhaps require us to rethink our concept of life in that in Gaianist thinking an ability to self-regulate (rather than respire or reproduce) is regarded as the distinguishing mark of life.

The way in which the planet is thought to regulate conditions to sustain life is a familiar one to us in geography and depends on the idea of feedback.

One of the observations that brought Lovelock to his conclusions (and serves to illustrate the general principle of self-regulation) was the discovery that over many millions of years the heat output from the sun had increased to a level that should have made the Earth too hot for life. However, Lovelock suggests that as the Earth heated up, plants evolved and spread over the Earth taking in carbon dioxide from the atmosphere, so cooling the Earth by allowing more outgoing radiation. Vegetation provided the necessary 'feedback' to control the Earth's temperature. Because the feedback process involved a reduction in temperature (rather than bringing about a further increase in temperature), we refer to this as *negative feedback*. The use of this terminology can be confusing in that we tend to associate the term 'negative' with bad or harmful situations. We might argue though that the reverse is true and that negative feedback processes stop things from getting out of control.

The Gaia hypothesis then proposes that living organisms and the physical components of the Earth are involved in complex interactions which maintain an environment that enables life to continue despite changing conditions. You may be wondering by now what all this has to do with geography fieldwork! If we go along with the Gaia hypothesis (and it is by no means universally accepted), there are three ways in which it may be relevant.

- The web of interconnections which constitute Gaia – between people, animals, vegetation, atmosphere, soil, rocks, rivers and oceans – emphasises the need to take a holistic view even though to be manageable our particular study may focus on a small set of relationships.

- If we are studying an environmental issue and are trying to predict the consequences of change, we may need to accept that the complexity of feedback mechanisms and our incomplete understanding of them casts a shadow of doubt over our predictions.

- If our studies involve us in considering different environmental values, Gaia theory offers a very much more robust and resilient view of the Earth than the 'fragile' Earth image projected by many environmentalists. Gaianism accepts the inevitability of environments changing and evolving but in ways that sustain life in the broadest sense, not necessarily the *anthropocentric* (people-centred) sense.

The Gaianist view could be interpreted as some sort of 'polluters' charter' by assuming that whatever abuses humans inflict upon the planet, the Earth will bounce back and regulate itself. Not quite so, say some Gaianists. If human activity threatens life on Earth then Gaia will respond by eliminating the human species to allow life in the broader sense to continue:

> *Any species (that is any part of Gaia) that adversely affects the environment is doomed; but life goes on . . . Gaia is not purposefully antihuman, but so long as we continue to change the global environment against her preferences, we encourage our replacement with a more environmentally seemly species.* (Lovelock, 1979)

The view of an Earth that is beyond complete explanation, understanding and prediction, is re-inforced by ideas emerging from the theories of chaos (Gleick, 1987). The essence of this theory is that very subtle differences in initial conditions are thought to result in large and, in part, unpredictable responses. The often quoted popular example of chaos in action is the notion that the movements of the wings of a butterfly might set in motion a train of events in the atmosphere which culminate in the formation of a hurricane.

The relevance of ideas about chaos to our investigations through fieldwork are twofold. First, we should not be at all perplexed if we discover things which we cannot explain – the complexities of all the interacting mechanisms involved may preclude the explanation of many phenomena. Secondly, we may need to challenge people who make excessively certain predictions about the consequences of changes to the environment. This should apply as much to oil companies that try and tell us that dumping their disused equipment at sea is perfectly safe as it does to environmental groups who predict ecological disaster from such actions. Often we do not and cannot know, in which case it may be prudent to adopt what is called the *precautionary principle*. This strategy proposes that where there is uncertainty about the outcomes of some change in the environment, interference should be avoided.

Nature- or people-centred views of the Earth?

Many people express a concern for the future of the Earth, its resources and its inhabitants including ourselves. But opinions as to how we

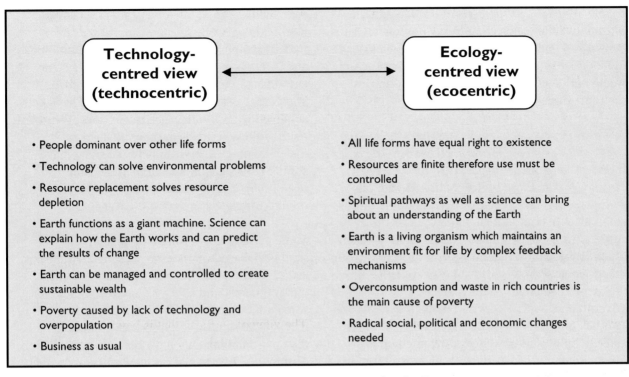

Technology-centred view (technocentric)	Ecology-centred view (ecocentric)
• People dominant over other life forms	• All life forms have equal right to existence
• Technology can solve environmental problems	• Resources are finite therefore use must be controlled
• Resource replacement solves resource depletion	• Spiritual pathways as well as science can bring about an understanding of the Earth
• Earth functions as a giant machine. Science can explain how the Earth works and can predict the results of change	• Earth is a living organism which maintains an environment fit for life by complex feedback mechanisms
• Earth can be managed and controlled to create sustainable wealth	• Overconsumption and waste in rich countries is the main cause of poverty
• Poverty caused by lack of technology and overpopulation	• Radical social, political and economic changes needed
• Business as usual	

Figure 2.1   Environmental viewpoints – a spectrum of values and attitudes.

should live and make decisions about the environment differ widely. It has been proposed that attitudes about the relationship between the Earth, its resources, other living things and ourselves tend to arise from a number of different world views. There is no single environmental viewpoint and much has been written about the subject. Eckersley (1992) distinguishes no less than sixteen variations of environmentalism. For our purposes this obviously needs simplifying. Most positions on environmental matters can be grouped into one of two major world views – the technology-centred (technocentric) and the ecology-centred (ecocentric). Figure 2.1 attempts to summarise these positions as involving two ends of a continuum.

The technocentric view

Central to this outlook is the idea that technology can keep pace with and provide solutions to environmental problems. When some resources become depleted, alternative resources will be discovered to replace those that have become scarce. The Earth and its complex processes are regarded as being comparable to a great machine which can be understood and controlled through scientific research. Given sufficient knowledge of how the Earth functions, its behaviour can be predicted and managed through appropriate policies to provide wealth and comfort for the human species.

Problems of world poverty tend to be viewed in terms of human numbers exceeding resources, so focusing solutions on population control. These approaches favour a 'business as usual' outlook, with no fundamental changes in economies and society being necessary. It is believed that governments and manufacturers can apply science and technology to make the necessary adjustments to overcome environmental problems. The sorts of policies that come from this way of thinking are things like fitting catalytic converters to cars to try and reduce air pollution, or constructing underground bunkers to store nuclear waste. This position also tends to be a people-centred outlook and normally regards the human species as being more important than other life forms.

The ecocentric view

Ecocentrism differs from the technology-centred view in several important respects. Most fundamentally, the human species is regarded as having status and rights more equal with other living things with whom we share the planet, and it is believed that endangered species and landscapes have inherent rights to exist.

It is recognised that the rate of resource use is very uneven between rich and poor countries. It is considered that the Earth has both insufficient resources and a limited capacity to absorb waste to enable all inhabitants to consume at the current rates prevalent in rich countries. Consequently it is considered that global development policies need to be directed towards reducing consumption and waste in rich countries, to allow poor countries their fair share of the Earth's resources.

A version of ecocentrism, sometimes labelled the *deep* or *dark green approach*, takes these ideas further. Deep greens suggest that the 'outer ecology' of the Earth is closely linked with our own personal 'inner ecology'. An example of this is the idea that our attitude to nature and the Earth springs from our attitude to ourselves and to each other. If we exploit other people or are exploited by other people then this leads to ways of behaving that exploit and abuse nature. Because governments, workplaces and perhaps schools and families often have a hierarchical structure where some people exert power over others, then this favours patterns of behaviour which exploit more generally. These patterns are then reflected in our attitudes to nature. So, it is argued, social, political and personal changes are needed in order for people to build a right relationship with the natural world.

A consideration of different environmental perspectives (see Job, 1995a) is almost inescapable if you are involved in issue-based fieldwork where different individuals or interest groups adopt different viewpoints on environmental matters.

**Ways of knowing and understanding –
science or senses?**

In recent years geographers have often framed their investigations around the scientific method following a structured sequence of steps (see Chapter 3). This sort of approach is based on ways of thinking that appeal to our powers of reasoning rather than to our emotions and feelings. It is a convenient and reassuring structure as it provides a simple sequence of steps rather like a recipe. Just as a recipe should enable us to produce perfect puddings, following this method should enable us to produce perfect projects. But the recipe is only as good as the ideas, tastes and judgements of the person who created it and does not allow much scope for our own creative flair, spontaneity or different tastes.

This approach has become so dominant in our way of thinking that other ways of knowing and understanding have all but been forgotten. Perhaps

we need to remind ourselves that the scientific method is only one of many approaches to understanding and interpreting our surroundings and is a relatively recent one. In more ancient cultures than our own, understanding and knowledge of environments appears to have been achieved without reference to any sort of scientific methodology or measurement. Instead, an understanding of environments seems to have sprung from accumulated experience and responding to surroundings through the senses, often through living very close to nature.

Some geographers brought up on a diet of fieldwork based on measurement and hypothesis-testing feel that while their carefully organised measurements and analyses have brought about some understanding of how things work in a mechanical sense, the essence and wholeness of the environments they have been studying and the distinctive character of particular places have somehow escaped them. There is a growing sense that places and environments have a meaning and importance beyond what can be measured and quantified. While we can carefully measure the biomass in all the trophic levels of a forest and model the cycles of energy and nutrients within it, the essence of that forest may still elude us. It is not until we lie on our backs staring up into the sunlit canopy or bury our faces in the moist litter and breathe in its rich humic aromas or embrace the massive girth of the ancient oak or sleep beneath the foliage and hear its mysterious nocturnal sounds that we really experience the essence of the forest through our senses. While our measurements may help us to understand some of the processes taking place within the forest ecosystem, it is probably more through our senses that we come to care and feel deeply about its well-being.

Since we are accustomed to interpreting our surroundings largely through reasoning rather than our senses, we may have broken the connections with the Earth that enable us to experience it through our senses. For this reason, Chapter 4 includes some ideas for reawakening our sensory experience of environments.

It is not that we would wish to reject scientific explanation as a means of trying to understand the Earth. It is rather that there is a need to recognise both the achievements and limitations of scientific explanation while opening the way for other means of knowing about the Earth based on our senses, feelings and emotions. A writer on educational concerns in relation to the environment summarised this idea in the following way (McDonagh, 1986):

> *We need to tell children a new story about the universe, based upon what we know from science but also imbued with the wonder and mythological colourings that are the natural offspring of reverence.*

While a sense of wonder is something we may experience in our geographical explorations, not everyone will feel happy with the idea that our activities should involve reverence for the places we visit. For many of us brought up on a diet of scientific explanation of the Earth, such ideas may seem rather pagan. Perhaps, though, if we reflect on how other cultures before us and elsewhere on the Earth have interpreted nature without the help of our sort of science, we can begin to accept that there may be more than one pathway to understanding. Furthermore, we cannot escape the uncomfortable observation that science-based investigations of the Earth have often been used to mistreat rather than revere it, while cultures with closer spiritual connections with nature have often tended to treat the Earth with more care.

Here and there – local to global

Following on from ideas about wholes and parts it is easy to see how local studies almost invariably have a global dimension. A study of air pollution in a neighbourhood may have a local significance in terms of the health and well-being of people in the immediate community, including ourselves. Yet the cocktail of emissions which we may detect can drift with the wind and interact to contribute to ground-level ozone pollution and acid rain in distant places. Similarly, not all the pollutants we detect locally have been generated in the immediate vicinity. Consider an investigation of coastal management which may include options for sea defences using large timbers or resistant rocks. Timbers sufficiently hard and massive to withstand the ravages of the sea are unlikely to be found outside a mature tropical rainforest, while the thousands of tonnes of igneous boulders for the rock revetment are going to leave a mighty hole in the cliffed flanks of some Hebridean island. In small ways we could go on to argue that the forest felled to provide the timber defences is no longer taking up carbon dioxide from the atmosphere, which in turn may contribute to climate change, sea level change . . . and aggravated coastal

erosion! This sort of feedback thinking may enable us to see how intended solutions may ultimately contribute to the problem.

Building out the links ties our local case study inextricably to distant places and often to global economies and climates and to distant cultures and ecosystems. Recognising and pursuing these links can give added significance and value to our locally-based studies.

Fieldwork for a change – asking critical questions

Let us consider the following examples of project titles which are typical of many issue-based field investigations of recent years:

- Which is the best location for the new superstore?

- Which is the best route for the motorway?

- Which river valley should be dammed to create a new reservoir?

These are the sorts of questions that geography students have often asked and sought to answer through field-based investigations. They are what we might call *locational* questions in that they involve comparing different sites and investigating how those different places might be affected by changes. They involve physical environments and people and in many respects are sound geographical questions. They are the sorts of questions that geographers have often collected information about in order to assist planners and developers to make choices between alternative locations.

The weakness of these sorts of questions lies in their inability to include any critical thinking about the fundamental nature of the development under consideration or any search for alternatives. Because developments like superstores, motorways and reservoirs are such a familiar part of contemporary landscapes, it is easy to fall into the trap of thinking of such changes as not only inevitable but desirable indicators of a developing society and economy. But as soon as we move from a reductionist view to a holistic view we begin to see that the indirect repercussions of such developments may have a range of far-reaching consequences beyond the immediate vicinity of the site. As soon as we apply ecocentric rather than technocentric thinking we see a world in which nature is subdued, controlled or degraded and landscapes which once combined nature and people but are now transformed to managed technoscape. If we move from an investigation where only the measurable things count to one that embraces beauty, wilderness, fairness and conviviality, our questions and conclusions go way beyond decisions about the locations of developments. If we are dealing with changes to environments that have the potential to degrade the landscape, squander resources or deprive or divide human communities, then there may be more important questions to ask than simply where such developments should be located.

By asking narrowly framed locational questions there is no encouragement to explore the demand side of resource issues, only the 'where' of the supply side. For example, alternative strategies to water resource use which recognise the finite nature of the resource and ways of reducing demand, are unlikely to be considered in an investigation of which valley should be flooded to make the next reservoir. Similarly, the social causes and resource consequences of rampant consumerism need never be explored in a study that is only concerned with where the next superstore should be located.

The preceding sections have tried to summarise a number of recent changes in thinking which impinge on how we view the world.

The next chapter begins by looking back on the evolving approaches to fieldwork in geography, distinguishing strengths and weaknesses and considering some established styles of fieldwork in relation to the changing world views.

Suggestions for further activities

- For a piece of fieldwork you have been engaged in, consider what links could be made between the place or topic you studied and the wider world.

- For each of the following local fieldwork investigations, find three ways in which each might be related to wider global issues:

  – a study of the effects of a proposed by-pass
  – a study of a coastal flooding issue
  – a study of the impacts of a new windfarm.

- Without referring back to the text, try jotting down your own understanding of the following:

  – the Gaia hypothesis
  – a holistic view of the world
  – chaos theory
  – reductionism
  – postmodernism.

  Then check your understanding with the glossary facing page 1.

- With a friend, discuss the main differences between technocentric and ecocentric views of the Earth. Which relates more closely to your own view, and why?

3 Evolving approaches to fieldwork

- *What was geography fieldwork like 30 years ago?*

- *Why did geographers start measuring things?*

- *Why values matter in fieldwork*

Introduction

This chapter sets out to review the different
approaches that geographers have adopted in
undertaking fieldwork. Each section begins with a
diary extract describing an experience of each style
of fieldwork, followed by a consideration of what
purposes are achieved by each approach. To some
extent the sections are arranged chronologically in
that they represent an evolving set of snapshots of
geographers at work in the field over a time-span
covering several decades. There is no intention to
offer judgements about the 'right' or 'wrong' ways
to go about fieldwork. The aim of this review is to
present the different strategies and then to consider
their strengths and weaknesses with respect to the
many different purposes (both geographical and
educational) which have been attached to
fieldwork. The final section puts forward a strategy
for fieldwork which draws on several elements of
established practice, and combines them into a
sequence of steps which aims to meet at least some
of the changing perspectives identified in Chapter 2.

Field excursion – the traditional approach

An example from Sussex (1967)

*Armed with cloth-bound copies of the one-inch to
the mile OS map, our stoutly-bound field
notebooks, pencils, Abney level and the purple
outlines of banda copies of base maps on
clipboards, we made a brisk ascent of the South
Downs escarpment. Led by our jovial and tweed-
clad teacher, we emerged from the autumn mists of
the Cuckmere valley into brilliant sunshine and
clear views north across the clay vale to the
sandstone ridges of the High Weald.*

*It was a revelation to compare the enormity of the
Wealden landscape to the cross-section diagrams
of the denuded anticline which we'd copied from
the meticulous diagrams in coloured chalk on the*

*blackboard the previous week. Now here was the
real thing with upstanding ridges and escarpments
exactly as they should be in relation to the
structure and strata of underlying rock. This was
the first in a series of grid-referenced sets of field
notes which we jotted down as our teacher
alternated between descriptions and explanations
based on his perceptions of the landscape, and
probing questions to encourage us to see what he
saw. So began a lifelong pleasure in reading
landscapes – perceiving shapes, colours, textures
and relationships in the landscape and thinking
about why, how and when. The process of
sketching the view across the Cuckmere gap to the
outline of the escarpment on the far side focused
our wandering thoughts, while labelling features
began to show us how human features of landscape
were closely linked to the physical geography.*

*Rivers, farms, villages, soil profiles and coastlines
all received similar treatment over the next three
days and it was not until the final day that we set
off in groups of three to accomplish transects
across the chalk escarpment from coast to clay
vale. The measurements and observations were
routine and repetitive, but with a growing sense of
independence and adventure and a growing ability
to interpret landscape, we began to feel like real
geographers.*

Prior to the quantitative revolution of the late
1960s, the sort of activities described above
provided the dominant experience of fieldwork for
many students of geography. Those of us of
sufficiently advanced years, who are of a nostalgic
disposition and find it difficult to jettison
possessions from the past, may be able to unearth
field notebooks from 30 or more years ago whose
contents reveal something of the nature of the field
excursion. If we were fortunate to have been
guided through the landscape by a skilled
practitioner who took care to ensure that
observations and detail were carefully recorded,
we might open a bound notebook whose pages

14

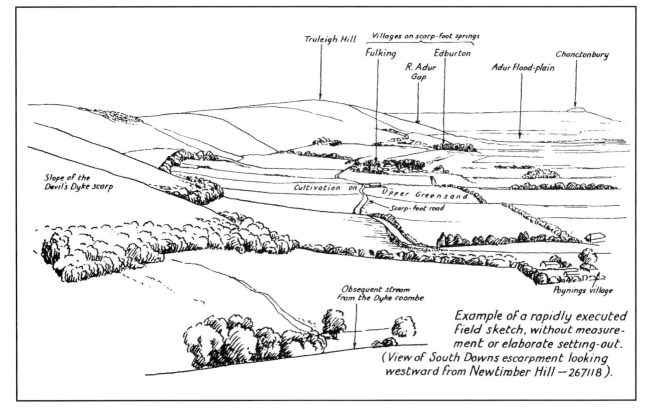

Truleigh Hill Villages on scarp-foot springs
Fulking   Edburton   Chanctonbury
R. Adur
Gap   Adur Flood-plain

Slope of the
Devil's Dyke scarp

Cultivation on Upper Greensand
Scarp-foot road

Obsequent stream
from the Dyke coombe   Poynings village

Example of a rapidly executed
field sketch, without measurement or elaborate setting-out.
(View of South Downs escarpment looking
westward from Newtimber Hill — 267118).

Figure 3.1   An example of geographical landscape drawing.
Source: Hutchings (1955)

recorded in notes and sketches something of the essence of the landscapes we were exploring. Places would have been carefully grid-referenced then described in what today would be considered a somewhat holistic and integrated manner. A record of the landscape as a *palimpsest* would often emerge, with geology and structure as the underlying influence but bearing mantles of soil, vegetation and human use both past and present.

Locations might well have been organised in the form of a transect, perhaps from north to south across Purbeck in Dorset or the Weald of Kent and Sussex, or from east to west across one or other flank of the Pennines, in order to bring out regional diversity and landscape change across a variety of underlying geological formations. Variation in landscape was often regarded as a key attribute for a suitable fieldwork locality, as implied in the following definition of this type of fieldwork:

> *The examination and analysis in the field of an accessible piece of countryside showing one or more aspects of regional differentiation.*
> (Wooldridge and East, 1951)

Landscape descriptions would be illuminated with the pencilled outlines of annotated field sketches,

the execution of which developed skills in observation, recording and interpretation.

Geoffrey Hutchings (Hutchings, 1955) provided us with superb examples of geographical field sketching, or 'landscape drawing' to use his preferred terminology. He describes the aim of such undertakings in the following terms:

> *A geographical drawing, however limited its content, should render the landscape features faithfully, and be so annotated, that it could be used by another observer as a guide or key to the view . . .*

Figure 3.1 shows an example of his work.

The landscape tradition in geography has been reaffirmed by Professor Goudie in the following terms:

> *. . . landscapes are one of the greatest gifts to humankind. Landscape has a great potential to stimulate interest in Geography in the young and in the lay person, but is also an area where human and physical geographers can liaise to produce a coherent story.*
> (Goudie, 1994)

Among the purposes achieved by this long-established approach to geographical fieldwork we might identify:

- an integrated view of landscape in which human features and physical elements are linked and interrelated

- development of a sense of place through an appreciation of how interacting sets of factors combine to bring about landscapes with their own individual characteristics

- developing skills in landscape literacy, map reading, sketching and recording of information

- an implicit sensitising to landscape aesthetics.

The process of the traditional approach to fieldwork might be summarised in the sequence of stages outlined in Figure 3.2.

It is easy to criticise the traditional field excursion from a present-day viewpoint of how learning ought to take place. Students adopted a relatively passive role; the field leader was seen as the all-knowing provider of knowledge. Landscapes were

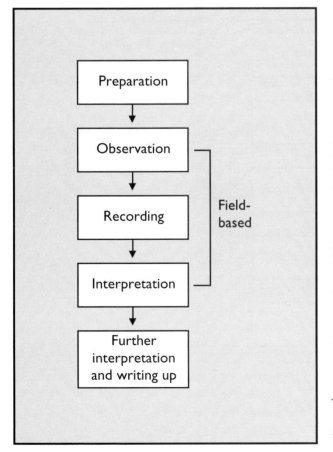

Figure 3.2   A traditional approach to fieldwork.

interpreted somewhat uncritically, as if they were devoid of environmental, social or political conflict. But for those who experienced this type of fieldwork, most would recall the pleasure and satisfaction of acquiring the skills to 'read' and interpret a landscape in its wholeness and thereby to grasp something of the essence of place.

As approaches to geographical fieldwork based on measurement rather than observation began to infiltrate, a number of criticisms were expressed which it was felt could be overcome through quantification. These included the following.

- Observation of a landscape could not in itself explain the complex of causal factors which formed it.

- Identifying a sequence of stages in the development of a landscape overemphasised the role of physical factors, tending to imply that human features developed primarily in response to physical factors. This viewpoint, sometimes referred to as *environmental determinism*, has been criticised for giving insufficient attention to the role of cultural, political and social factors in shaping the human landscape.

- Relationships between factors in the landscape were assumed from observation without rigorous testing.

- Simply developing skills in observation and interpretation was felt to be insufficiently demanding intellectually.

By the late 1960s the scene was set for the quantitative revolution to transform the experiences of geography students in the field.

Made to measure – fieldwork for the quantitative revolution

Somerset 1974 – a spot of Davis bashing

'Tomorrow we're off for a spot of Davis bashing' announced the young Scots tutor with a gleeful twinkle in his eye. As the new recruit to the field centre I was due to observe some established fieldwork days before leading my own courses. This all sounded rather different from the rather passive field sketching and note taking of my A-level geography field course not many years previously.

We started in the lab with the instruction that today's study would focus on rivers and how they worked. 'What happens to the velocity of a river as it flows from source to mouth?' we were asked. The dominant view was that it would get slower. Why? Because of a gradual decrease in the long-profile gradient, was the popular suggestion. These predictions became the basis for our hypotheses, though some dissenting voices suggested that other factors might be involved. The roles of turbulence, bed roughness, channel shape and discharge were also discussed and alternative hypotheses proposed on the basis of these other factors. Two rather different models of the river system emerged, one based on the Davisian, time-dependent model of youth, maturity and old age, the other based on a systems approach of channels adjusting to some sort of equilibrium state.

It was time to subject our hypotheses to rigorous field testing. Shiny flow meters, tapes, metre rules and dumpy levels were flourished and their use explained before hurriedly loading into an old bus and making for the headwaters of a nearby drainage basin selected for study. Fortunately the field recording sheets had neat boxes for recording all the measurements we'd referred to in our hypotheses and we proceeded downstream, bundling, out of the bus at intervals to record a set of data in increasingly deep and seemingly fast-flowing river channels – the Davisian model was already looking shaky.

On return to the field centre a frantic number-crunching session yielded a large data set, with river sites forming the rows and channel variables the columns. Graphical plots and correlation coefficients enabled rigorous testing of hypotheses which were finally related back to the two models of fluvial processes. Finally generalities concerning the applicability of dynamic equilibrium ideas to fluvial systems was discussed. There was a certain satisfaction in the iconoclastic tumbling of long-treasured ideas through our own findings.

The approach adopted here has been described elsewhere as *field research* (Everson, 1973) and represented the adoption by geography of methods widely used in the sciences. You may come across different diagrams to illustrate this process of field research – two variations are offered in Figures 3.3 and 3.4. In both examples, the core of the process involves the development of hypotheses –

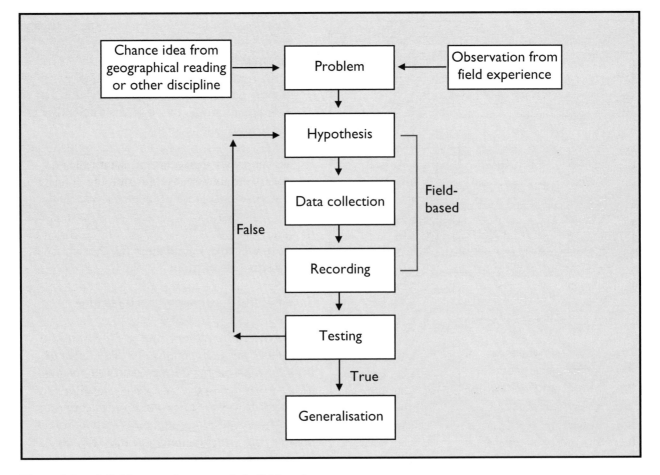

Figure 3.3   A field research approach to fieldwork.

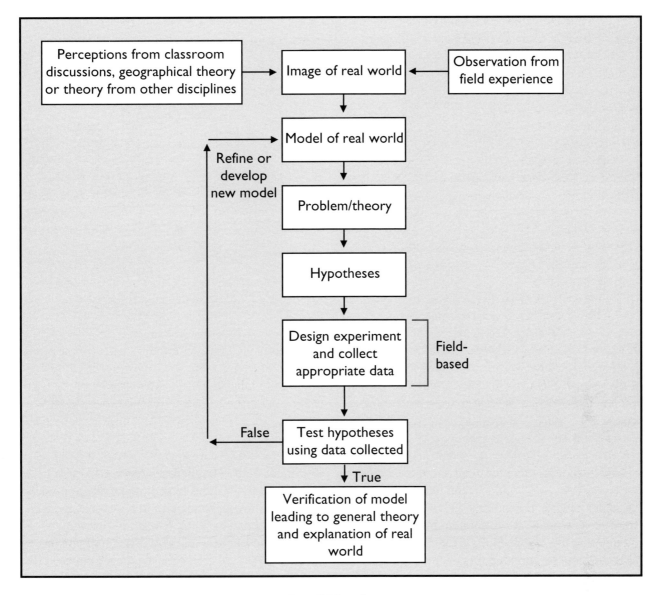

Figure 3.4   A modified field research approach to fieldwork.

statements and explanations about phenomena in the field which we suspect to be true – followed by the collection of data about those phenomena. A testing process, normally involving data collation, presentation and analysis, entails comparing findings from the field with the expected hypothetical pattern or relationship. Hypotheses are then either confirmed or rejected. Rejection requires returning to earlier stages in the model in order to generate fresh hypotheses which in turn might require further data collection.

So far it would appear that the development of fieldwork practice around hypothesis testing was brought about by the introduction of quantitative methods into geography as a whole. This is partly true but there were other interesting changes happening in both geography and education that reinforced the dominance of hypothesis-based approaches to fieldwork. Particularly in physical

geography, systems theory was being applied more widely, emphasising the interconnections and relationships between the variables which make up a physical system. Some systems models emphasised the flows of energy and materials – in the river basin, the hill slope, the soil profile or the ecosystem, for example. Other models focused on the relationships between sets of interacting factors in relation to a particular physical environment. The fieldwork experience of river work in Somerset, for example, was based on a model similar to that in Figure 3.5 where the boxes contain the variables and the linking lines show assumed relationships, either positive or negative. This sort of model lends itself very readily to hypothesis testing. The model can be developed as a collective effort, based on reading, previous observation or logical thinking. Each link in the model can then be expressed as a hypothesis, for example: 'As the hydraulic radius increases, the

18

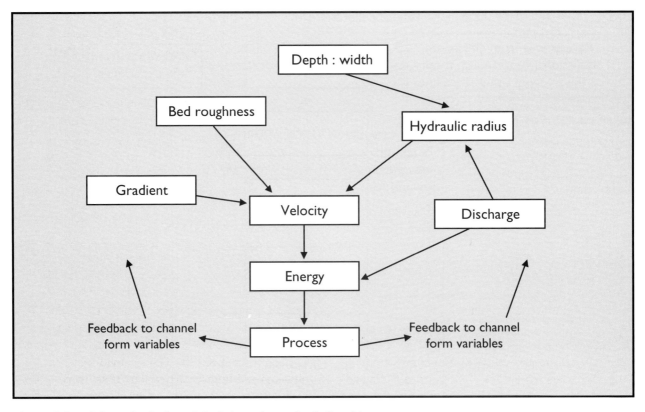

Figure 3.5   A hypothetical model of river channel relationships.

channel becomes more efficient and the velocity increases'. A system with several interacting variables can be broken down into a series of testable statements. It is important to remember though that this is essentially a reductionist approach and by adopting this method, we are assuming that by looking at all the individual links, this will contribute to an understanding of the whole system. The river model in Figure 3.5 illustrates a simple limitation of such reductionism. If we have velocity data for a number of sites along a river we often attempt simple statistical correlation with other channel variables which we think might affect river velocity (e.g. hydraulic radius, gradient, channel roughness). In reality, all these factors may well be interacting collectively and in a sense cancelling each other out to give fairly uniform velocity along a river. Thus an upland stream with low efficiency, high bed roughness and a steep long-profile gradient, might end up with a very similar velocity to a lowland river with a much lower gradient but greater efficiency and lower bed roughness. Yet in our analyses we often apply bivariate statistical methods (such as Spearman's rank correlation) which can only compare two variables at a time.

So systems thinking as well as the introduction of quantitative methods went hand in hand with the widespread application of hypothesis testing as the dominant fieldwork approach. As well as being stimulated by changes in geography, the approach also found favour in relation to how ideas were developing in education. It was felt that the traditional field excursion involved students in a relatively passive role, observing landscapes under guidance and responding to questions to which the teacher already had fairly fixed ideas as to the appropriate answer. Hypothesis testing offered the potential for more active participation in the field and considerable control over the direction of the field investigation, if students were given the freedom to participate in the process of hypothesis generation from their own perceptions.

In practice, though, often to enable equipment and recording sheets to be sorted out beforehand, the process of hypothesis generation was, and often still is, closely stage-managed towards hypotheses that are predetermined. In reality, the 'active learning' is often confined to the process of using field equipment and data collection.

A significant consequence of adopting hypothesis testing as a basis for fieldwork was its emphasis on establishing generally applicable theories about patterns and processes in the landscape rather than emphasising the uniqueness of particular places. The special features of a particular river, for example, became less important than establishing theory about how rivers in general behaved. Hypothesis testing thus encouraged what is sometimes referred to as the *nomothetic* (or law-seeking) approach in geography. As discussed earlier, an overemphasis on seeking generalisation may be partly responsible for the decline in the place-unique (or *idiographic*) tradition in geography. Fieldwork based too exclusively on data collection may therefore fail to stimulate in us a sense of place and a feeling for the special character and quality of particular landscapes. Whilst it is possible to develop a sense of place alongside data collection, there is a tendency to imagine that the sorts of activities that help develop place sensibility – sketching, contemplating, discussion, meditation – are somehow inferior to the more rigorous tasks of measurement and data gathering.

If we consider some of the emerging viewpoints outlined in Chapter 2 it could be argued that hypothesis testing is more fundamentally flawed. Hypotheses are frequently focused on the relationship between two variables which leads to neat manageable studies but unless the hypotheses are placed in a wider context, investigations are likely to be narrow and reductionist with no attempt to relate to the broader scene. Furthermore, since the testing of hypotheses normally relies on quantitative data, experiences in the field which don't yield measurable data are undervalued and may pass unrecognised. Over-reliance on hypothesis testing may therefore be constraining if we are interested in developing more holistic world views and if we value sensory experience as a valid means of discovery and understanding. If hypotheses are developed prior to field experience, we also tend to remain detached from them – they fail to involve us personally. This is particularly so if we draw our hypotheses from theoretical models in textbooks or simply 'borrow' a hypothesis from a previous piece of fieldwork.

Yet many geographers feel an attachment to the method – it is familiar and offers a clear guiding structure to an investigation. It has a distinctive beginning, a middle and an end, and leads to tangible results, thereby promoting confidence and reassurance. There are possible modifications to the approach which can overcome some of its constraints. For example, if we undertake some discovery or exploration of the field environment before generating hypotheses and collecting data, this helps to ensure that the hypotheses we generate are based on our own questions, arising in turn from our own experiences of places. Rather than ditching hypothesis testing as a basis for fieldwork, Chapter 4 proposes a fieldwork model which retains it as an option within a broader framework.

By the late 1970s some geographers were beginning to look beyond hypothesis testing as the dominant fieldwork approach, or at least exploring ways of incorporating it into a less restrictive framework. This was in response to a range of growing doubts about an excessive concern with measurement, often seemingly for its own sake. Geographers were beginning to think about the purpose of all their quantitative studies. Were they relevant to real-life problems and issues? Hypothesis testing often focused on studies of purely academic interest, with little or no direct application to practical problems in the real world, while the integration of physical and human geography which characterised the traditional field excursion had been lost. This separation of physical and human environments seemed increasingly problematic as awareness of environmental problems grew, and it became evident that human activity and the physical environment were closely interdependent. There was a growing need to turn attention to the effects of human decisions on the environment, and this introduced a new priority into geographical study. Increasingly, geographical investigation began to focus on environmental and social issues. This new emphasis provided a potential purpose and relevance to fieldwork which hypothesis testing *per se* had often lacked, as well as helping to heal the rift between physical and human geography. The application of geographical study to *issues* introduced a new element.

An issue involves a question or problem over which there are different viewpoints, even perhaps conflict or dissent as to the preferred course of action. Having taken on issues as a focus for investigation, geographers then needed to involve themselves in the origins of these different environmental and social viewpoints and therefore developed an interest in the values which different people held and the more specific attitudes and opinions that arose from those underlying values.

It is this emphasis on issues, often involving consideration of people's values, together with an interest in students being more in control of their investigations, that distinguishes an approach to fieldwork which has come to be known as *geographical enquiry*.

Figure 3.6   Students investigating wind energy issues.

Geographical enquiry

A case study in mid-Wales – 1993

As the little train from England rattled down between steep wooded slopes towards Machynlleth we became aware of some curious additions to the landscape. The bare windswept summits above the valley were punctuated by tall steel towers, each supporting a rhythmically rotating blade like some outsize propeller from an old-fashioned aircraft. It was no longer just sheep that were being farmed on these upland plateaux. As well as turning grass into meat and wool, the wind too was being harnessed to feed electricity into the national grid. Our initial responses rather favoured these futuristic additions to the landscape. They seemed to offer a reassuring glimpse of a future in which we could go on enjoying the comforts and convenience of plentiful electricity without warming up the planet or polluting land and rivers with acid rain, or running short of finite energy resources. The windy heights of mid-Wales, where traditional farming, we were to discover, was so economically precarious, seemed to be the ideal environment for such development.

It was not until later when we began to hear of conflicting local opinion that other viewpoints about windfarm development became evident. Feelings were running high, it seemed, with strong views being expressed at planning enquiries where permission was being sought for further sites to be developed. Some voices talked of infuriating droning sounds from the turbines, others of the risk the rotors might pose to rare birds of prey. Hill walkers spoke of the intrusive impact of windfarms on wilderness landscapes. Others, perhaps inspired by a concern for the culture and well-being of the region, spoke of the profits from windfarming draining away to financial institutions and corporations outside Wales, rather as the region had been bled of the riches from its minerals, water and timber resources. Several landowners, though, were keen to cash in on the substantial payments being offered by the generating companies. Clearly we had an issue on our hands. 'Should further development of wind power be permitted in the region?' became the key question for a group enquiry.

This extract describes the starting point for the process of a geographical enquiry. There are obvious differences between what took place here and how many hypothesis-based field investigations often begin. First, the focus of the enquiry can be described as being an issue in that it involves changes to an environment about which there are conflicting viewpoints. Secondly, it obviously has a relevance both to the local environment and to a wider global context encompassing energy, climate change, pollution and sustainable development. Thirdly, it brings together physical and human geography and provides opportunities for applying a wide range of geographical methods. It is also firmly rooted in a particular place whose distinctive landscape, economy and culture are highly relevant to the issue being debated.

The extract above only describes the initial stage in the process of enquiry. The full sequence of stages is outlined in Figure 3.7. This is a simplified version of the now widely used 'Route to Enquiry' published elsewhere (Naish *et al.*, 1987). Having identified an issue, in this case from some chance observations but informed by a more general awareness of energy and environmental matters, it can be seen that the enquiry follows two parallel tracks, one focusing on factual material, the other concentrating on people and their differing viewpoints. The two pathways come together at the end in a process of personal decision-making.

Factual enquiry more objective data ←---	Route and key questions ----	Values enquiry ---→ more subjective data
Becoming aware of a question, issue or problem to do with people and their environment.	**OBSERVATION AND PERCEPTION**	Becoming aware that there are different views about the question, issue or problem.
Define the question, issue or problem, decide what information you need then collect and describe the information.	**DEFINITION AND DESCRIPTION** **What? and Where?**	Gather information about the values, actions and statements of different people involved.
Analyse the information then interpret it to try and reach explanations. Is any more information needed?	**ANALYSIS AND EXPLANATION** **How? and Why?**	Compare the opinions people hold with the results of your factual enquiry. Is anyone distorting the facts through bias or prejudice?
Using your explanations and understanding, try to predict what would happen if different decisions were taken.	**PREDICTION AND EVALUATION** **What might?** **What will?** **With what impact?**	Who holds the most power and so will have the greatest effect on decisions? What are other possible decisions and would any of these be preferable?
What is the most likely decision and what are the likely effects on the environment and people?	**DECISION-MAKING** **What decision?** **With what impact?**	What will be the responses of those who hold different views from the decisions taken by the more powerful people?

PERSONAL EVALUATION AND JUDGEMENT
What do I think? Why?

Which of the viewpoints do you support in this issue? What decisions and actions would you favour? How would you justify your preferred course of action?

PERSONAL RESPONSE
What next? What shall I do?

Decide whether to try and change things through direct or indirect action and/or through changes in your own lifestyle and decisions.

Figure 3.7 Issue-based fieldwork using the route to enquiry.

In this particular study the factual enquiry centred on field surveys and interviews with windfarm managers to determine the potential of a sample area for wind energy production. This involved detailed anemometer surveys to identify suitable sites for windfarm development, followed by estimates of power output and financial return both to landowners and the generating companies.

The values enquiry identified several groups of people, individuals or organisations involved in the issue. These included landowners who would receive annual payments for each turbine sited on their land and the generating companies and financial institutions who stood to make substantial profits if planning permission were granted for new sites. It also included other local people who feared noise pollution and visual intrusion and conservation bodies who opposed further development on grounds of damaging impacts on the landscape. It was predicted that the influence held by the generating companies and their backers and encouragement by government departments who were trying to meet targets on limiting carbon dioxide emissions would lead to more windfarms being built against the wishes of some local people and hill walkers.

Individuals who carried out the enquiry came to a number of different personal decisions. There were those who felt inclined to support further development because of beneficial global effects while others felt the turbines should be owned and operated by local people rather than large corporations. There was also some feeling that any form of electricity generation had harmful effects so policies should concentrate on conservation and using less rather than developing new technology to generate more. It soon became evident that these different views on this specific issue could be related to the range of environmental opinion represented by the ecocentric–technocentric spectrum (Figure 2.1). Lively debate ensued between the 'ecos' and 'technos' on a range of other environmental issues.

Geographical enquiries such as the one outlined here overcome several of the problems identified with narrowly focused hypothesis testing. The approach also takes account of several of the emerging viewpoints identified in Chapter 2. It encourages us to feel personally involved in our enquiries, it is easier to see your own local study in a wider world context and it accepts that there are valid interpretations of the world which relate to personal values and do not depend purely on science and measurement.

Geographical enquiry has generally led to more exciting and relevant forms of investigation which often have the potential to contribute to change towards a better world. In practice, however, some difficulties remain, among them the following.

• Factual enquiries involve predicting the consequences of different decisions. If we adopt the views that the Earth may not be a predictable machine (as discussed in Chapter 2), there may be considerable uncertainty about our predictions.

• There has also been a tendency for many geographical enquiries to be insufficiently critical of the nature of environmental change. As outlined in Chapter 2, key questions which only ask where a development should be located may fail to see change in a sufficiently broad and critical context.

• In practice, a tendency has persisted to base enquiries on past projects or second-hand ideas rather than on personal experience of an environment.

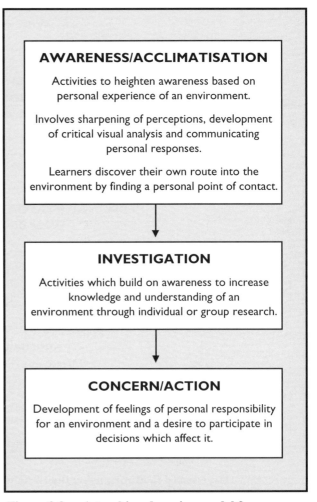

AWARENESS/ACCLIMATISATION

Activities to heighten awareness based on personal experience of an environment.

Involves sharpening of perceptions, development of critical visual analysis and communicating personal responses.

Learners discover their own route into the environment by finding a personal point of contact.

INVESTIGATION

Activities which build on awareness to increase knowledge and understanding of an environment through individual or group research.

CONCERN/ACTION

Development of feelings of personal responsibility for an environment and a desire to participate in decisions which affect it.

Figure 3.8 **A teaching–learning model for outdoor experience.**
Adapted from Hawkins (1987)

• It may be difficult to reach a personal decision without a clear view of one's own values in relation to environmental and political matters.

The last two of these problems may well be linked in that unless you feel that the starting point for your enquiry involved you personally and came from your own experience, then one tends to remain somewhat detached from the whole process. If you feel personally involved from the start, then you are more likely to want to translate your findings into action and perhaps become an agent for change.

To lead us into the next chapter, which considers ways of making connections with your field environment, let us examine a further model which has been put forward to help us feel some ownership of our investigations. It is a relatively simple structure involving three stages and is summarised in Figure 3.8 (based on Hawkins, 1987). The initial stage acknowledges that each of us has a unique view and interpretation of an environment and the important thing is finding your own way in. What is it about that place which sparks your interest and arouses *your* curiosity? Before following up the most obvious things which could lead to rather superficial studies, we might need to delve beneath the surface and uncover some of the more subtle aspects of the place. As

we will explore in the next chapter, there are things we can do which can sharpen up our sensitivities, open up fresh perceptions and help us adopt more critical perspectives. This initial stage of discovery is sometimes described as *acclimatisation*, a process of getting in touch with and feeling comfortable in a new environment, or perhaps seeing a familiar environment from a fresh perspective. Having found our own point of contact, we might then move through to more structured investigation. This might take the form of geographical enquiry or, if appropriate, hypothesis testing. In either case, although we are likely to focus on particular 'parts' of the environment for investigation we will first have had a vision of the 'whole'.

The third box in this model is rather similar to the final two stages of the route to enquiry (Figure 3.7) in that it concerns reaching personal decisions and acting upon those decisions. To have meaning, this stage requires a context. Imagine perhaps that you have undertaken an ecosystem survey of habitats on the site of a proposed superstore. You have surveyed and mapped the spring flowers in the meadow. You have recorded the purple orchid in one of your quadrats, the sparkling droplets of morning dew glistening on the petals. In a sense you have become a part of that meadow and that meadow a part of you. You have formed your own

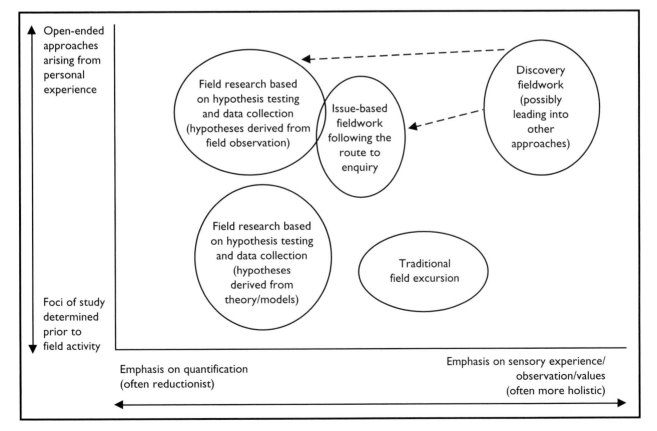

Figure 3.9   Graphical representation of fieldwork approaches.

judgements about the relative priorities of meadow and shopping scheme. You are emotionally and personally a part of that issue. Important personal decisions then need to be considered – whether to take personal action and, if so, what sort of action.

Figure 3.9 attempts a graphical summary of the approaches outlined in this chapter by considering each style of fieldwork in relation to two distinguishing themes, represented by the two axes of the graph. The horizontal axis concerns the extent to which a fieldwork approach relies on measurement and data collection and the degree to which it draws on more qualitative forms of experience. It would be wrong though to assume that the two are mutually exclusive, as the latter may be used to feed into the former. The vertical axis concerns the starting point and focus of investigations. Have they arisen from your experience in the field or were they predetermined by someone else or by geographical theory? You may not agree with the positions in which different approaches have been placed. Restructuring this sort of diagram can be a useful source for debate.

In the next chapter an approach is offered that draws on established approaches to fieldwork while attempting to incorporate some more innovative activities which reflect the new viewpoints identified in Chapter 2. The emphasis will be on ways of enhancing the process of discovery in order to lead into more meaningful and personally derived investigations.

Suggestions for further activities

• Consider a piece of fieldwork which you have undertaken recently. To which (if any) of the approaches outlined in this chapter did it correspond most closely? If a different approach had been adopted, how might the fieldwork have been organised?

• Go to a local viewpoint. Make a field sketch and annotate it using the sort of labels that Hutchings might have used (see Figure 3.1). Add further annotations to identify features in the landscape which might form foci for geographical enquiry.

• Consider the three pieces of fieldwork described in this chapter. Which would you most like to have been involved in in terms of:
  i) enjoyment
  ii) value in terms of geographical understanding
  iii) value in terms of acquiring new skills?

4　From personal experience to investigation

- *Making connections with place*

- *Literature as geography*

- *Stimuli to discovery*

Introduction

Rather than aiming at the bull's eye, fire your arrow where you will, then draw the target around where it lands.

The review of approaches in Chapter 3 illustrates the richness and diversity of traditions in geographical fieldwork. Drawing on some of the changing world views from Chapter 2 and some of the limitations of existing approaches identified in Chapter 3, a number of new strategies might be identified for a fresh approach to fieldwork. These include:

- allowing the starting point of our investigations to arise from our own experience of an environment

- attaching equal value to our feelings about places and events as to factual or quantitative information

- focusing on areas of environmental concern

- developing a sense of place.

Connecting through the senses: the contribution of deep ecology

It is perhaps a little optimistic to imagine that on going to a new environment we will spontaneously become aware of its attributes and opportunities for fieldwork. This may also apply to familiar places closer to home. Thinkers from the deep ecology movement suggest that we have become increasingly cut off from stimuli coming from the natural world, particularly the more subtle or slowly changing aspects of our surroundings. Our perceptions are more tuned in to the sorts of rapidly changing, often brightly coloured images of the city, the sorts of stimuli which reach their extreme expression on the computer game video screen – a very different perceptual experience to

watching the rhythmic but subtly varied motions of breaking waves on the shore. An interesting test of our awareness of and integration with our surroundings is to try answering the sorts of questions listed below. These have been adapted from a quiz (Where are you at?) put together by some North American deep ecologists.

Where are you at?

This is a self-scoring test on basic environmental perception of place. The quiz is culture bound, favouring rural dwellers over city dwellers. Scores can be adjusted accordingly.

1. Trace the water you drink from precipitation to tap.
2. How many days until the moon is full (plus or minus a couple of days)?
3. Describe the soil around your home.
4. How did the culture who lived in your area before you gain their livelihood?
5. Name five native plants in your region and their season of availability.
6. From what direction do winter storms generally come in your region?
7. Where does your garbage go?
8. How long is the growing season where you live?
9. Name five trees in your area. Are any of them native?
10. Name five resident birds in your area.
11. What is the land-use history of your region over the past 100 years?
12. What geological events/processes have influenced the landforms where you live?
13. What species have become extinct in your area?
14. What is/would be the climax vegetation in your area?
15. From where you are reading this, point north.
16. What spring wildflower is among the first to bloom in your area?
17. What rocks and minerals are found in your region?

18. Were the stars out last night?
19. How many people live next door to you? What are their names?
20. How much fossil fuel do you use each week?

(adapted from Devall and Sessions, 1985)

The example here is designed for use in the home environment. A modified version could be compiled for use in an area where you are going on a field trip, then try to answer the questions on arrival and again at the end of the visit.

The purpose of a quiz such as this is not so much to achieve a high score as to reflect on how in touch with our surroundings we are and to act as a stimulus to re-establishing lost connections. It is usual for most people to obtain very low scores, signifying the degree to which modern living has disconnected us from real awareness of things natural and the life support systems upon which we depend.

Several imaginative ideas for raising our sensory awareness of our surroundings have been developed in environmental education and by deep ecologists. The following sections offer examples of activities that use sensory experience to make connections with our surroundings which might then be used as a springboard for more formal geographical investigation.

Haiku poetry

Haiku is a simple three-line poem (of Japanese origin) consisting of seventeen syllables. A balanced form is achieved through having five syllables in the first and last lines and seven in the middle line. An enjoyable but somewhat facetious example is sometimes recited by the punk poet, John Cooper Clark (to be read in a Salford accent):

> *To convey feelings*
> *In seventeen syllables*
> *Is very diffic . . .*

The process of haiku writing as a means of raising awareness of our surroundings might involve the following steps:

Find a place to sit for ten minutes which feels comfortable enough to allow you to relax. Clear your mind and allow stimuli from your surroundings to come into your mind (visual, sounds, smells). To stimulate the senses you could use a blindfold for the first five minutes to increase awareness of sounds and smells. Taking off the blindfold may heighten visual responses when you remove it. What was the first thing you noticed after you took it off? At the end of the ten minutes jot down a dozen words – sights, sounds, smells and feelings. Begin to arrange these in a haiku structure.

This can be an individual activity or a collective endeavour with one person gathering a collection of words from the whole group then orchestrating a communal haiku.

Here are some examples, created (by geographers, which is why the syllables are not quite as they should be) in a variety of environments:

> *Swirling green water*
> *Flows endlessly on to the*
> *Limitless ocean*

> *Your time here is short*
> *Thinks the round golden pebble*
> *In rhythmical waves*

> *Fumes from a taxi*
> *Swirl round the face of the child*
> *As she sleeps unaware*

The common feature of these haiku poems is that they arise from personal experiences in the field and incorporate emotional responses to those environments. A personal connection is established which may encourage you to find out more about those environments and perhaps, also, care more for them.

Making connections through literature

Reading passages of prose or poetry by other writers in an appropriate environment can have profound effects in terms of making contact with an environment. Here are two examples.

Mountain Pass

> *Over this small brave road, the wind blows.*
> *Tree and bush are left behind, only stone and*
> *moss grow here. Nobody has anything to look*
> *for here, nobody here owns anything, up here*
> *the farmer has neither hay nor wood. But the*
> *distance beckons, longing awakens, and*
> *through rocks, swamp and snow, they have*
> *provided this good little road, which leads to*

*other valleys, other houses, to other languages
and other men.*

*At the highest point in the pass, I stop. The
road descends on both sides, down both sides
the water flows, and everything that is side by
side up here finds its way down into two
different worlds. The small pool that touches
my shoe runs down towards the north, its water
comes at last into distant cold seas. But the
small snowdrift close beside it trickles toward
the south, its water falls toward the Adriatic
coast down into the sea, whose limit is Africa.
But all the waters of the world find one another
again, and the Arctic seas and the Nile gather
together in the moist flight of clouds. The old
beautiful image makes my hour holy. Every
road leads us wanderers too back home.*

(from *Wandering* by Hermann Hesse, 1920)

This sort of writing does not come from people
who would normally be described as geographers,
yet their writing is strongly geographical. What
more eloquent description of the hydrological
cycle could you find than this? When read in the
field, perhaps on a mountain pass or on any water
divide between two catchments which drain away
to different places, a feeling of connection with the
water cycle can be experienced. The circulating
processes of the water cycle are used here as a
metaphor for the human experience of setting out
on a journey and returning home. This sort of
writing which draws parallels between
geographical experience and inner feelings can be
very powerful and memorable, especially when
read in an appropriate location in the field.

But how might such an experience lead us into
more conventional geographical investigation? We
might begin by thinking about the different
environments that the two trickles of water will
experience. Will both retain the purity of their
early beginnings? How might each be affected by
human activity in the catchments? Do the channels
retain their naturalness or do they become
controlled and managed, and with what
consequences? We are perhaps going to be more
interested in the answers to these questions if they
have arisen from a personal experience that has
touched our emotions. We may also care more
about the outcomes of our findings.

We might draw upon other literary sources which,
while touching our emotions in a similar way to
Hesse's description, are more overtly geographical
and can lead us very easily into investigations of

issues. Here is an example from the Welsh poet,
R. S. Thomas.

The Welsh Hill Country

*Too far for you to see
The fluke and the foot-rot and the fat maggot
Gnawing the skin from the small bones,
The sheep are grazing at Bwlch-y-Fedwen,
Arranged romantically in the usual manner
On a bleak background of bald stone.*

*Too far for you to see
The moss and the mould on the cold chimneys,
The nettles growing through the cracked doors,
The houses stand empty at Nant-yr-Eira,
There are holes in the roofs that are thatched
 with sunlight,
And the fields are reverting to the bare moor.*

*Too far, too far to see
The set of his eyes and the slow phthisis**
*Wasting his frame under the ripped coat,
There's a man still farming at Ty'n-y-Fawnog,
Contributing grimly to the accepted pattern,
The embryo music dead in his throat.*

* = lung disease

R. S. Thomas

Reading this powerful piece of writing while
sheltering from the weather in a ruined farmhouse
in the Welsh mountains can be a deeply affecting
experience. It certainly strips away any romanti-
cism we might have about hill sheep farming and
conveys strong emotions about the human impacts
of rural depopulation. It locates us – spatially,
historically and culturally. We are not just
anywhere. This is Snowdon not Swindon, we are in
a desolate upland place with a culture, a people, a
history and a physical geography all of its own.

We might follow up such a reading by devising and
acting out a short drama focusing perhaps on a
family leaving their upland farm after generations
of occupation.

In dipping into the realms of literature and drama
in these ways we have ventured a little beyond the
conventional boundaries of geography but with a
legitimate purpose in mind. We have built a
personal and emotional link with the place we are
to investigate as geographers and by doing so we
may bring greater understanding and meaning to
our subsequent endeavours. More specifically,
such experiences may help us to develop a more
holistic view of an environment in which some of

the many connections to other places, other times and other voices can be appreciated. While our study may well need to be more focused than this, it will at least ensure that our investigation is set within a wider view and that our senses are engaged as much as our analytical skills.

If our investigation leads into an issue-based enquiry, we are more likely to feel personally involved and show care and concern for the place we study if we feel connected to it through our senses. Experiences that engage our senses are perhaps more powerful than other experiences we may have in the field, based on more structured investigation involving logic and analysis.

The art of discovery

A distinction needs to be made between the purely sensory experiences described above and the process of discovery. So far we have not been thinking particularly in geographical terms about our surroundings, and our activities might not be described as directly geographical. To bring us closer to geographical investigation yet still allowing our experience of a place to generate the focus for more investigative work, we might embark on a process of discovery. The following passage describes the experience of a teacher attending a course who was determined that the focus of his endeavours should come from the environment he was in, not from any preconceptions or dictates from other people.

In the summer of 1984 I joined a group of environmental educationists for a study conference in the French Alps. As part of the proceedings it was decided to attempt a 24-hour transect of an alpine hamlet, each investigator taking a different perspective which ultimately would be synthesised. At the centre, scientists enthusiastically chose such topics as soil temperatures or stream flow, the geographers, aspect or plant distribution. I rather frustrated my colleagues by refusing to choose anything despite the exhortations that I 'must'. When we arrived at the alp my companions began organising their equipment whilst I strolled off and sat on top of a nearby hill, gazing down on the small flower rich meadows. . . . I was enthralled by the environment in which I found myself. I was becoming aware of it and waiting to discover my own way into it. . . . I walked down to one of the fields and caught sight of a

magnificent blue round-headed rampion growing on a nearby slope. I didn't know what it was at the time – it didn't matter – but I knew that here was my 'way in'. My response was initially a sketch, then some photographs, then a poem, and then and only then did I begin to wonder what it was and why it was there. This led me into aspect, soils, rock-types, water availability and botanical keys . . . I had built a personal relationship with the environment and gained knowledge and understanding of it. Above all it had become a part of me, and I a part of it . . . (Hawkins, 1987)

This passage illustrates the process of discovery. It allows the place we are in – its landscapes, its rocks, its life forms, its buildings, its people – to speak to us. It may be though that on entering an unfamiliar environment we are not equipped with the necessary receptive equipment to pick up the more subtle messages, especially if we are less practised at observing and interpreting landscapes than the author of the passage above.

The following ideas are intended to assist the process of discovery by sharpening our awareness of places. They are not intended to form the core of an investigation. They are appropriate to either a familiar or an unfamiliar environment. Even in a familiar environment, its very familiarity means that much may pass unnoticed or we fail to appreciate the full significance of things we do notice.

Using stimulus cards

A more structured approach to stimulating our perceptions of a familiar or unfamiliar environment is to use sets of cards similar to those illustrated in Figure 4.1. These have been compiled primarily with the exploration of a rural environment in mind. Further examples for use in an urban environment are included in Chapter 6. These consist of focusing questions or tasks which can guide us towards noticing elements of the landscape which we might otherwise miss, or encourage us to think about our surroundings more deeply or in relation to wider issues. Some encourage us to express our feelings and make aesthetic judgements, others are more analytical and strictly geographical. Some focus on imagining how the environment has changed over time. It does not especially matter at this stage whether we come up with the right answer, and in many cases there may be no right answers.

29

Figure 4.1   Some examples of stimulus cards.

Focusing on smaller things

In wandering through the landscape our attention is normally focused, at least initially, on the broad view and larger features, yet many significant processes and some of the most beautiful natural phenomena occur at the micro-scale. This is especially true if our inclinations are towards the study of ecosystems, soils, rocks or weathering. Botanists are accustomed to spending large amounts of time on their hands and knees and geographers may well benefit from adopting a similar posture. It is therefore recommended that the next activity is carried out in the 'botanist's position' – nose close to the ground and bum in the air. Begin by randomly exploring the surface beneath your nose, perhaps with the aid of a magnifying glass. Take a 2 or 3 metre length of string and begin to arrange it along the ground in the form of a nature trail. The route will therefore take in interesting or beautiful features, the positions of which could be marked with twigs or numbered mini-posts. Imagine you are designing a nature trail for an ant. Try to think beyond the objects themselves to the processes they may be involved in: the decomposing leaf with its skeleton of lacy veins; the encrusting lichen with its hyphae penetrating the weathering rock; the discarded ring-pull from a can of drink (in relation to the decaying leaf?). All have meanings and significance beyond their existence as objects on the trail, meanings which may throw up deeper questions or themes for subsequent investigation.

Tools for discovery

It is worthwhile considering taking some of the following with you, either to sharpen perceptions or help retain experiences that you may want to reflect on later:

- OS map
- Notebook and pencils
- Sketchbook and/or camera
- Any copies of old photographs or old maps of the area (this focuses our attention on environmental change)
- Portable audio cassette recorder, either for recording natural sounds or conversations (Video cameras can be useful but they can easily dominate your attention to the exclusion of other experiences. They can also create barriers between yourself and people you meet.)
- Binoculars
- Magnifying glass

Some guiding questions

It may be useful to apply some of the following 'focusing' questions:

What is this place like? What distinguishes it from other places you know?
What does it mean to me?
What does it mean to the people who live here?
How is it related to other places?
How did it use to be?
How might it change?
Are there differing views about change in the locality?
How would we prefer it to change?
Can it go on like this?

Talking to people

We are very accustomed in more structured geographical investigations to conducting questionnaires to find out people's views on specific matters. In the discovery process of an investigation we need to adopt a more relaxed and open framework for relating to people we encounter, encouraging them to talk about where they live and what it means to them, without imposing our own view of what we think is important.

Secondary sources for exploring environmental change

We may well wish to pursue specific secondary sources as part of our more focused investigation but there is also a lot to be said for undertaking a fairly unstructured review of source material about a locality as part of the discovery process. Local history libraries or county record offices are rich sources of written, photographic and mapped information about places, particularly from a historical perspective. If equipped with computerised searching facilities which enable you to type in key words, this will speed up the process of finding information about particular places or particular themes. Here are some of the resources you may come up with which can offer snapshots of both the physical and human landscape at past dates.

- Trade directories (e.g. Kelly's Directory). These were published often annually throughout much of the nineteenth century and through the early years of this century on a county basis. The information is normally arranged on a parish basis with a description of the parish at that date, census data and an inventory of all individuals in the parish engaged in trade activities. More detailed guidance is offered elsewhere in the interpretation of these directories (Job, 1988).

- Victoria County Histories. These large volumes were published on a county basis at the end of the nineteenth century and contain a wealth of information as well as decennial census data for the nineteenth century. If you come across old photographs or maps, try to obtain copies and take them with you into the field for the purpose of present-day comparisons.

- Early editions of Ordnance Survey maps at various scales, and thematic maps (geology, land use, vegetation).

- If at all possible, consultation of aerial photographs and satellite images of your fieldwork area will provide new perspectives and show patterns and change which are indistinguishable from a ground-level view. A

useful source of information on the interpretation of remotely sensed images as well as sources of such images can be found in Barnett *et al.,* 1995.

From discovery to investigation

The activities described in this chapter could be regarded as ends in themselves. They could lead in many directions – to artistic representations of places, dramatic presentations, political campaigning, expeditions. In the context of this book, though, they are designed to lead us into more structured geographical investigation, but based on experiences which engaged us personally and in doing so perhaps also touched our emotions.

The following two chapters, one set in a coastal environment (Chapter 5), the other set in city environments (Chapter 6), describe activities which involve personal connection and discovery that then lead into more structured geographical investigation. The process of moving from discovery to investigation is explored in the context of the coastal and urban case studies.

5 Fieldwork case studies from the South Devon coast

- *Connecting with the coast*

- *Key questions from personal experience*

- *An investigation using hypotheses*

- *An investigation using enquiry methods*

Introduction

This chapter offers examples of fieldwork in the context of a specific environment. The approach follows the sequence of steps outlined in Chapter 4, working through from ideas of sensory connection and discovery, then drawing on these subjective experiences to lead into more structured investigations. Two contrasting examples of investigations are described. The first is an example of fieldwork based on hypothesis testing, and the second focuses on geographical enquiry applied to a current issue. While the intention is to exemplify and contrast general approaches to fieldwork which can be applied in any environment, there is also the intention of conveying a sense of place and bringing out the unique character of the locality. Figure 5.1 shows some of the main features of the coastal environment in south Devon which features in this chapter.

Connecting

In Chapter 4 some of the advantages of finding your own way into an investigation through your own experiences of an environment were considered. It is difficult to plan this stage of an investigation. It depends on getting to know a locality, doing some background research, being open to the stimuli it offers and the people you encounter, and perhaps also trying to experience the place in different weathers and seasons, by day and by night.

I spent a long time studying the beaches of Start Bay in South Devon, both as a researcher surveying its changing morphology, comparing its present form to past records, applying theories of wave action to try and explain its ever changing

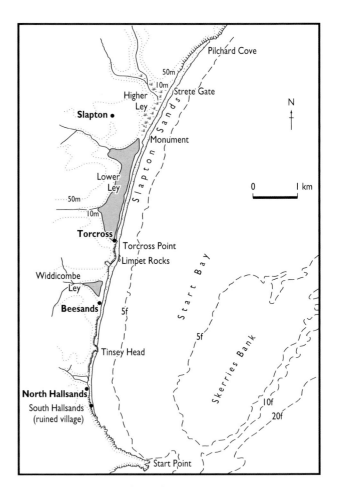

Figure 5.1   Map of the Start Bay coast.

features, as well as leading groups of students there on geography field courses. I came to realise that much of this investigative work was rather detached and somehow separate from my feelings about the place, and it was only more recently that the scientific investigation and sensory experiences began to come together.

As the embers of the fire glow dim, we crawl into the warmth of our sleeping bags and the moon casts a silvery shimmer over the bay.

Lowering my head onto a folded sweater for a pillow and drawing the sleeping bag over one ear and cutting out the sound of waves on the lower shore, I'm surprised to still hear the soft rhythmic rush of moving pebbles on the wave washed lower shore, the sound apparently coming up through the beach beneath my head. A realisation grows that these hushed vibrations which are finally picked up by the small bones in my ear before passing to the brain represent the final dissipation of a distant energy source beyond the earth. Before sleeping I try to trace back the sequences and phases through which this energy has passed. The first (or rather the last) stage is fairly straightforward and close at hand. Breaking waves wash the shingle at the shoreline to and fro then vibrations set up by these movements pass through the beach from pebble to pebble to reach the stones beneath the folded sweater which forms my pillow. The night is calm yet the waves still break on the shore. It must be that the disturbance of the ocean's surface which formed these waves happened in windier parts, perhaps far from this shore. And whence came the wave forming winds? My thoughts turn to the mighty towering weather systems over the North Atlantic, the different systems of high and low pressure which spawn the wave making winds. I think to the strong heat of distant tropical places and the low sun of northerly climates and how these differences in temperature sow the seeds for the building of the pressure systems. Then thoughts turn to the solar energy zapping through space and the tiny fraction which reaches our atmosphere. A feeling grows of being connected – not only to this beach and the sea and the waves, but to all the shores of the earth who share this single huge ocean. Thoughts of the sun as the source of the energy which, after several transformations, moves and shapes the pebbles on the shore and the moon as the force driving the massive tidal heavings of the sea makes connections also to the huge blackness above and its myriad points of bursting energy.
(Diary entry, the author, August 1994)

It may not be immediately obvious how such an experience, with its emphasis on emotions and somewhat abstract thought, relates to fieldwork. Reflecting back to some of the issues raised in Chapter 2 where we identified the need for new directions in fieldwork, there are a number of ways in which an experience such as that described above might lead us into more investigative fieldwork.

- Establishing a personal and emotional connection with the place we are studying may motivate us to ask questions which lead us into more formal enquiry, while ensuring that those questions are arising from our own experience rather than being imposed upon us.

- Such experiences may help us to develop a more holistic view of an environment in which some of the many connections to other places and other times can be appreciated.

- If our investigation leads into an issue-based enquiry, we are more likely to feel personally involved and show concern for the place we study if we feel connected to it through our senses. It is more difficult to develop caring attitudes towards a place, its people and other life forms if we remain emotionally detached from them. Experiences that engage our senses are perhaps more powerful than other experiences we may have in the field based on more structured investigation involving logic and analysis.

Discovery

What follows is a collection of experiences in a particular coastal environment. As outlined in Chapter 4, the process of discovery involves actively seeking information and experience, and always being open to the unexpected opportunity.

'Chance favours the prepared mind'

Our discovery begins at Hallsands, a curious collection of ruined cottages resting precariously on a sloping platform of weathered rock a little above sea level. We had already discovered a little about the place from a series of papers written over seventy years ago which we unearthed in the local history library. Shortly after the village was ruined, Richard Handsford Worth recorded the events of a stormy night in 1917 in the Transactions of the Devonshire Association of 1923:

The seas broke green against the sea-walls, they swept across the village street and burst open the doors on the far side . . . Mr. George Trout was only able to save himself

*from being washed out of a house by
catching hold of the door jambs as he was
carried past them . . . The upper floors
presented their own particular
disadvantages, in that falling masses of
water broke down the roofs."*

We had with us copies of photographs of the village from before the storm. The place was scarcely recognisable but by identifying particular points of reference in the old photographs we were able to take photographs and draw sketches from the same points to make comparisons. From these we compiled lists of things which had changed, leaving us in no doubt as to the dramatic alterations in both the physical environment and human activity over the past eighty years or so. Most dramatically of all, the shingle beach which previously fringed the village and provided access to the bay was gone. Gone too was the evidence of previous human occupation – most of the cottages, the fishing boats and the washing lines festooned with flowing garments of another age. From the crumbling rocky platform which now supported the few remaining ruins, a precariously undercut cliff dropped to a wave-worn shore of deeply eroded grey rock.

From the ruined village we made our way to a small bay to the north where the crumbling cliffs give way to a short stretch of shingle beach. Again we had some old photographs which showed a very different scene from today. In the photographs half a dozen wooden boats were drawn up onto the beach just above high water and the shingle was strewn with equipment for fishing – things like big upturned woven baskets (which we later discovered were crab pots), long nets stretched out to dry, coiled ropes, anchors and groups of people chatting or working.

We got talking with a retired fisherman called Jim who told us how he used to make crab pots from willow stems cut from the marsh at the top of the beach. He reckoned he could see two of his cousins, now long since dead, in one of the old photographs, two tough-looking women called Patience and Ella, two of the Trout sisters. We had already seen their names on the foundation stone of Trouts Hotel on the clifftop above the ruined village. The inscription showed the letters 'O.B.E.' after Ella's name. We found out from Jim that she'd been awarded the O.B.E. after rowing out to rescue an African sailor who'd survived after his ship was torpedoed four miles offshore in 1917. On closer inspection the photograph showed two remarkably swarthy women, obviously accustomed to the rigours of salty winds, choppy seas and the handling of heavy fishing gear rather than light household chores. Their rugged appearance showed no attempt to conform to any conventional female stereotype, but their beauty rested elsewhere, in the selfless acts of bravery and determination in an often harsh environment which seemed to have characterised their lives (Figure 5.2).

We also discovered that some years before the storm which wrecked the village, a large amount of shingle had been dredged from the sea bed just offshore of the village. This had been loaded into dredgers and taken off to make concrete for the dockyard installations under construction in Plymouth. Local opinion was that the shingle beach which fronted the village was then drawn down to fill the holes left by the dredging, so leaving the village vulnerable to storm waves.

Miss Ella Trout, O.B.E.   Miss Patience Trout

Figure 5.2   The Trout sisters of Hallsands.

Figure 5.3   Nature's pie chart showing pebble frequencies on North Hallsands beach.

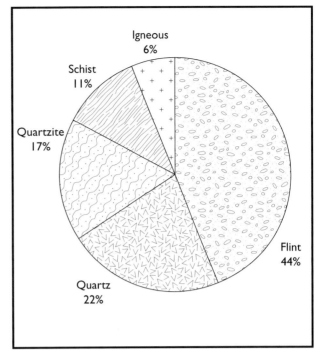

Figure 5.4   Computer-generated pie chart of pebble frequencies.

After our chat with Jim we skimmed pebbles across the calm steel-grey waters of the bay. With only the gentlest swell disturbing the water surface, it was hard to imagine the sea tearing down cottages and battering the cliffs. The flat grey stones which were scattered across the beach were ideal for skimming but not as beautiful as the smaller rounded pebbles, some with vivid colouring, which made up most of the beach. The shingle that looked a sort of uniform brown colour from a distance was varied and brilliantly coloured close to: wet and shining red pebbles with specks of white crystal, smooth pinky brown oval shapes, knobbly hard stones, creamy white or orangy brown – much more varied than the local cliffs that were a grey slaty stuff (called schist, we found out later) with veins of quartz running through. On closer inspection the schist was equally curious and beautiful with narrow bands of grey and white twisted and contorted into weird loops and waves, clearly the product of some previous violent contortions of the Earth's crust. Someone had the idea of collecting the different coloured pebbles and arranging them into patterns and representations of the landscape such as the field patterns on the hills above the cliffs. Later, as part of an investigation, we used the same technique to show the frequency of each type of pebble by grouping similar pebbles and arranging them on a flat slab of rock as a pie chart which we then photographed (Figure 5.3). There were interesting discussions after we produced a computer-generated version (Figure 5.4) as to which was the

more appealing representation. One further curiosity struck us before leaving Hallsands. Over part of the beach the shingle had been stripped away to expose a thick layer of a rather soft black peaty substance. Closer inspection showed fragments of wood and even the odd tree stump. Clearly, at some time in the past, vegetation, including trees, had been growing on what was now a shoreline regularly washed by the tides.

We walked on north over the next headland to Beesands. From the map we were expecting to find a long strip of shingle beach, but at the southern end in front of the village was a huge sea wall made of massive rocks and a curved concrete wall at the top to reflect the waves. We dropped into the Cricket Inn and on the wall was a photograph which showed a huge width of shingle in front of the cottages covered with huts and boats (Figure 5.5). Where had all the shingle gone, we wondered? Had it been dug out to make way for the sea wall or had it disappeared by some other means, leaving the village exposed and in need of protection?

A further walk over the next headland brought us to the main shingle bar of the Start Bay coast. From the top of Torcross Point it was a breathtaking sight: a great long, smoothly curving ribbon of shingle, washed by the sea on one side and sloping gently to the reedy fringes of the freshwater lagoon of Slapton Ley on the other. Compared with the beaches at Hallsands and Beesands, there seemed to be an abundance of

Figure 5.5   Beesands about 1910.

Figure 5.6   Beesands about 1995.

shingle here, though we were later to discover evidence of recent lowering and narrowing of the beach part-way along. Some old wooden posts which used to support an old jetty and which no-one could remember seeing before had recently become exposed as the beach surface had dropped. Indeed, concern was expressed that a storm over the coming winter months could break through the shingle ridge just north of the monument, draining the ley and severing the main road which links the villages in the vicinity to nearby towns.

From this collection of experiences our curiosity was aroused and important questions began to occur to us both about past and more recent environmental change. The idea began to grow that this place had not always been as it is now, that it changed with the seasons and the weather, and though seeming to be fairly natural, may well have been altered quite drastically by human interference. Most significantly, the shingle beaches, which appeared to have buffered the coastal zone from the ravages of storm waves in the past, were in several places but shadows of their former selves.

This loosely structured exploration of the Start Bay coast gave rise to a number of unresolved problems. We were struck by the great variety of colours, shapes and textures of pebbles making up the beach material. We noted that a lot of them did not seem to match the rock types we had seen outcropping in the local cliffs. The presence of remains of trees and vegetation apparently in the position where they grew on the shore led to thoughts about changes in sea level. We were struck by the remarkable differences in the dimensions of the beach when we compared old photographs with the present-day appearance of the coast. We noticed places where the top of the beach appeared to be eroding and encroaching on the land. We contrasted the natural stretches of shingle shoreline with their wealth of unusual plant species, with the concrete walls and alien boulders of the stretches where sea defences had been built. Were the beaches really still shrinking and if so, why? If recent management policies continued, would (and should) the whole coast become an engineered strip of concrete, steel and imported boulders?

With these often puzzling and controversial questions in mind we set about trying to identify some key questions, though in some cases we were not overly optimistic of finding the answers.

From discovery to key questions

After the largely unstructured experiences of discovery we needed to pause for a period of reflection. We first listed what was memorable about the day's observations and events, not at this stage in any order, but as a shared collection of memories:

- Ruined cottages at Hallsands
- Ella Trout's rescue
- Jim Trout's fishy yarns
- Multicoloured pebbles
- Flat grey skimming stones
- Sea walls
- Shingle dredging
- Crab pots
- Willows from the marsh

- Old tree stumps and peat beds on the shore
- Beesands sea wall
- Old Beesands – beach and fishing industry
- Disappearing beaches
- Slapton bar and ley – predictions of change
- Unusual foreshore plants.

From this random list of events, people, places and objects it is possible to see links and relationships, enabling the items to be grouped into common themes:

- The origins of the shingle and the formation of the coastline
- Changes to the coast over time
- The destruction of Hallsands village
- Coastal management and human modifications to the coast
- The people of Start Bay and their changing lives.

Not all of these themes may be geographical, but they are all important because they arose from our experience, they became part of our collective memory and therefore part of us, and they may give greater meaning to our geographical themes. Hallsands, for example, is a fascinating place geographically but its meaning to us is that much greater when we know that the Trout sisters lived there and we hear tales of their remarkable exploits.

We should acknowledge at this key stage in the process of geographical exploration that we are moving from a more holistic view of our field area to a more reductionist one. We are 'homing in' on something manageable, but since our starting point was holistic we can keep a light hold on the imaginary strings which link our focused study to the wider world and past events. At a later stage, once we know more about the detail, we can still draw the linking ideas back in again.

Each of these themes might generate one or more key questions which could become a basis for further investigation. Table 5.1 shows three examples of how groups of memorable experiences might feed through into themes, key questions and then investigations.

Investigation 1: The development of the Start Bay barrier beaches – an application of field research

The barrier beaches (or bars) of Start Bay, particularly Slapton Sands, are spectacular and rather curious features. This investigation seeks to

Table 5.1

Memorable experiences	Theme	Key question	Investigation
• Destruction of Hallsands village • Accounts of seasonal change • Wooden piles on Slapton beach • Old photographs • Old maps and surveys	Changes in shingle level over time	Are the beaches equilibrium or disequilibrium systems and what are the implications for coastal management?	*Factual enquiry:* comparative beach surveys to establish the pattern of change over time. *Values enquiry:* investigating attitudes to different forms of coastal management.
• Stories of the destruction of Hallsands • Old photographs • Tales of Hallsands inhabitants	The destruction of Hallsands village	Was the destruction of Hallsands caused by shingle dredging?	*Factual enquiry:* comparing shoreline changes with weather data and the timing of dredging operations *Values enquiry:* comparing the views of people involved.
• Multicoloured pebbles • Rocks in the cliffs • Watching waves • Fossil forest	The geological composition of the Start Bay shingle and the movements of coastal sediment	What is the origin of the Start Bay shingle barrier beaches?	Investigation to analyse: • shingle lithology • geological exposures • wave action and sediment movement • secondary data on Quaternary history.

account for their development through a fieldwork approach involving hypothesis testing. Figure 5.7 summarises the stages which in this example lead from memorable events during discovery activity to a structured investigation.

Forming a hypothesis

Initial awareness of these landforms is raised as soon as we look at a large-scale map of the area. Field discovery cannot help but arouse curiosity as to their development and origins. Knowledge of the way in which sediment can be transported along coasts suggests a likely mechanism. A possible explanation might therefore have involved longshore transport of sediment in sufficient quantities to form spits across the mouths of coastal inlets (now occupied by Slapton Ley and other smaller freshwater lagoons at Beesands and Hallsands) until the spits reached a high coast at the far side, forming a bar of sediment. This closed off the former inlets from Start Bay which then received water only from their catchments, so

becoming freshwater lagoons. So far this explanation remains hypothetical but seems possible given our observations of the landforms and our knowledge of coastal processes in theory. If such an explanation is valid we might expect to find that:

> *The lithologies (rock types) of the shingle match up with sources of sediment along the coast (either to the north or south, depending upon the direction of longshore drift).*

Other possible field testing might involve surveys to investigate the distribution of the shingle along the Start Bay coast, measurements of wave and wind directions relative to the orientation of the shore, and pebble-tracing experiments using coloured samples of sediment.

Experimental design and data collection

We then set about devising some methods of investigation which involved a range of primary

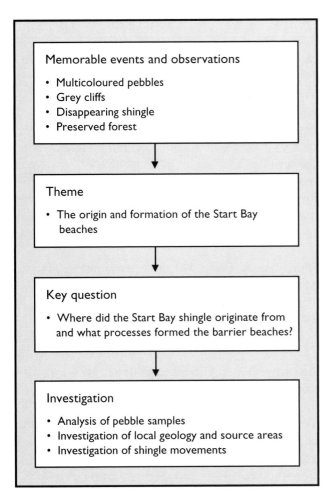

Figure 5.7   From memorable events to investigation – the origin of the Start Bay beaches.

and secondary information. A number of tasks emerged, the most important being:

a) collection and analysis of random samples of beach pebbles at intervals along the coast

b) examination of cliff exposures to give information about sources of material for the beach system, possibly supplemented by information from geological maps

c) observing wave direction to indicate the direction of longshore drift (though acknowledging that this might vary over time).

Careful practical attention to sampling methods and consultation of tide tables would be necessary prior to undertaking this fieldwork.

Data analysis and hypothesis testing

After grouping the pebble samples into rock types and counting the frequency of each, the results were plotted up as pie charts (Figures 5.3 and 5.4). The frequencies were then compared with the local geology map and field notes of rock types occurring in local cliffs. It soon became evident that only the few grey slabs of slate and schist could be easily traced to local cliffs, though the white quartz pebbles might also have come from veins in these cliff outcrops. Even so, eroded material from local cliffs could only account for about 25 per cent of the beach material at the most. The majority of the samples were found to be made up of the whitish-brown knobbly pebbles of hard flint, smooth pinkish pebbles of quartzite, sometimes with blood-red mottles, and scattered pebbles of variable colour containing angular crystals indicating an origin from outcrops of igneous rock. There seemed to be no obvious source for this diverse assemblage of multicoloured pebbles.

The high frequency of flints presented a particular problem in that the chalk rocks of Cretaceous age from which these hard knobs of silica are thought to have originated are characteristic of the distant cliffs and downlands of Dorset, Sussex and Kent, far to the east of this stretch of the Devon coast. But a glance at a map of the offshore geology reveals extensive outcrops of chalk on the floor of the English Channel – only some 30 km from the Devon coast. The pebble beds of Triassic age that the quartzites are thought to have come from can also be found outcropping on the sea bed even closer at hand. How could material have been eroded from these deepwater outcrops and transported to the beaches of Start Bay? At this stage our original hypothesis begins to look decidedly untenable.

Our understanding of wave processes tells us that the circulation of water within a moving wave only disturbs the surface layers of the oceans, so present-day wave action could not erode at the considerable depths involved. Furthermore, ocean currents, while able to transport fine sediment in suspension, do not normally have the energy to transport heavier sediment the size of beach pebbles. A possible alternative hypothesis might be put forward that the outcrops from which the flints and quartzites were derived could have been eroded at a time of low sea level during the last glaciation. Other sources of information suggest that about 10,000 years ago, towards the end of the last glaciation, the local sea level was thought to have been some 40 metres lower than at present, so the coastline would have been well to the south-east of its present position. Resistant fragments of rock such as the flint and quartzite eroded at that time might then have been transported landward as the ice sheets melted and sea level rose. Other evidence suggests that the shingle barriers were only swept up into their present positions about 2,000 years ago. This explanation suggests that the beaches are fossil landforms formed by past processes and that the shingle is not being significantly added to by present-day processes. Present-day wave action undoubtedly moves the shingle around (either north or south depending upon wave direction) but does not appear to be primarily responsible for the formation of the beaches.

Further reading (Hails, 1975) and field observations lend further support to this theory. The fossil forest beds which underlie the shingle barriers of the Start Bay coast have been dated to between 2000 and 3000 BP (BP = before the present, present = 1950) using radio-carbon dating techniques. When forests and later marsh vegetation were growing on what is now the foreshore, it might be assumed that the sea level was then lower. A rising sea level since then has driven the shingle landwards, burying the old forested coastline.

These sorts of conclusion, to some extent specific to Start Bay, have important implications for how coasts with beaches are managed. If it has been shown that much of the sediment has been introduced by past events such as the rising sea level as ice melted and the oceans warmed and expanded, then it is vitally important to conserve existing coastal sediments and not allow extraction for construction or other purposes.

Conclusion

A summary of this application of the field research approach is presented in Figure 5.8.

The rejection of the initial hypothesis in this study led to further development of alternative hypotheses which could be applied to the data already available. Although no new primary data was gathered, secondary material was used to help develop and support the modified hypotheses. As is often the case, a study that originally focused on a specifically physical theme yielded results with important implications for coastal management and decision-making. An investigation that initially seemed rather narrow and reductionist at the outset led to explanations which involved global climatic

changes, sources of sediment way beyond the field area, and events encompassing thousands of years of geological history.

The results of this sort of study should be treated tentatively, especially as past processes seem to have been involved which we cannot now test directly through fieldwork. Emerging views concerning the complexity of feedback mechanisms, ideas from chaos theory and the limitations of science, as discussed in Chapter 2, are further reasons for exercising caution in the interpretation of findings from fieldwork.

(Fuller contributions to our understanding of the Start Bay coast can be found elsewhere: Hails, 1975; Job, 1993a, 1993b; Robinson, 1961; Worth, 1904, 1909, 1923.)

Investigation 2: The Slapton line issue – an application of geographical enquiry

The following section provides a worked example of the route to enquiry approach to fieldwork using a live issue (unresolved at the time of writing) from the Start Bay coast. Figure 5.9 shows how memorable events from the discovery stage were fed through into investigation of an issue, while Figure 5.10 presents a summary of each of the stages in the enquiry as applied to this issue.

Observation and perception

Awareness of the issue arose from a number of field observations which suggested aggravated erosion along a stretch of Slapton 'line', the local name often given to the long strip of shingle barrier beach on the Start Bay coast. As described in the 'Discovery' section of this chapter, some stout old timbers were noticed near the middle car park, protruding from the beach surface. On enquiring from local people it seemed that these were the old supports for a wooden pier which had been driven into the shingle long ago. They had remained buried for many years until recent beach erosion exposed them. More recently, along the top of the beach, banks of fallen turf and soil had broken off the vegetated surface and rolled down onto the shore. If the shoreline was experiencing accelerated erosion, and if this were to continue, then undermining of the main road along the Slapton line seemed likely. The coast road links the towns of Kingsbridge and Dartmouth as well as providing access to Slapton village. Local people

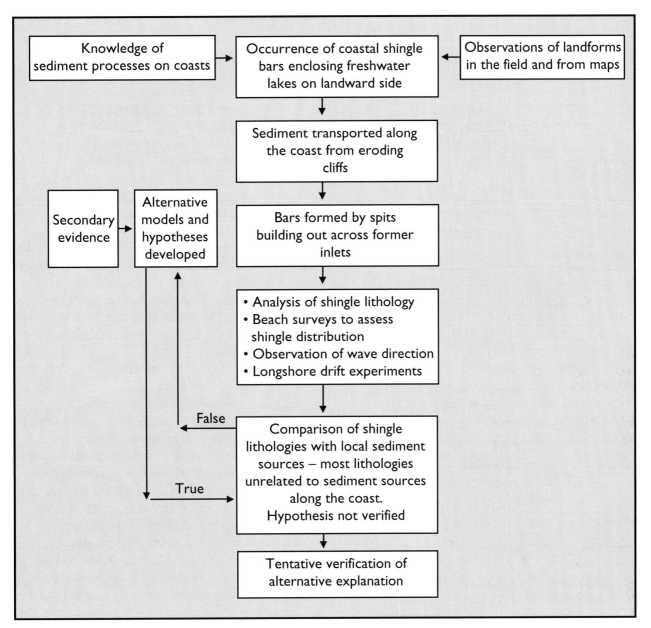

Figure 5.8   Field research methods applied to coastal fieldwork, Start Bay.

were already beginning to discuss the implications of further erosion and breaching of the road. There were a number of different viewpoints about what should be done.

Definition and description

A key question for the factual enquiry was put forward:

> *Is the beach in a state of equilibrium or dis-equilibrium and what implications do beach changes have for coastal management?*

To answer this question, a beach survey and map data were required to discover if beach levels and shoreline positions had changed significantly over time; and if erosion had occurred, whether it was continuing or had re-established stability. Records of past shoreline surveys were available against which present surveys could be compared (accounts of methods for surveying beaches are available elsewhere: Job, 1989).

These findings would provide some indication of the threat to the roadway. The values enquiry at this stage focused on enquiring into people's perceptions of beach erosion and what action if any they favoured. This involved both local residents and public authorities whose policies covered the coastal environment. In this example these included parish, district and county councils, the National Rivers Authority, the Ministry of Agriculture Fisheries and Food, and English Nature.

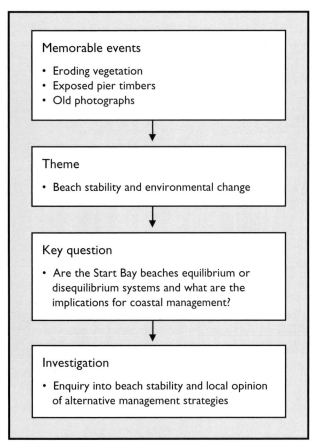

Figure 5.9   From memorable events to investigation of an issue – beach erosion at Slapton.

Analysis and explanation

A comparison of beach surveys at a number of sites over time showed that while shingle levels exhibited the normal seasonal pattern of lowering during winter storms and building during the summer months, the longer-term trend was one of decline. This was especially evident at the profile site closest to where erosion had first been observed. Here the shoreline had retreated some 30 metres between 1982 and 1995 and the beach surface was up to 4 metres lower (Figure 5.11). Detailed surveys at monthly intervals showed continuing retreat of the vegetated crest of the barrier, but some stability of the beach surface on the lower shore (Figure 5.12). The small eroding cliff cut into the shingle at the top of the beach was found to be advancing on the roadway at an average rate of 0.7 metres a month. If that rate were to continue, the road would be undermined in a year's time.

The values enquiry revealed widespread awareness of the problem but strongly varying opinions as to what action (if any) should be taken. Three main policies were referred to:

1. Extend existing sea defences (rock rip-rap and/ or concrete sea wall) to the threatened section of roadway.
2. Re-align the roadway by rebuilding the threatened section further inland (but still following the shingle barrier) and allowing erosion to occur.
3. Abandon the roadway along the line and use alternative existing roads and lanes.

The main impacts of these alternatives might be summarised as in Table 5.2 (page 45).

The possibility of abandoning the existing road and rebuilding along a new route to the west of Slapton Ley was also mentioned. Other possibilities include options such as beach nourishment to replace the lost protection resulting from beach erosion, and doing nothing, to see if the beach rebuilds naturally.

Prediction and evaluation

Factual and values enquiries begin to come together at this stage. If previously discussed ideas about the limitations of our ability to predict the outcome of human decisions on the physical environment are accepted then we must remain uncertain about the outcome of the different courses of action. Examples from elsewhere (including a local case at Beesands) suggest that sea defences might indeed restrict the landward advance of erosion towards the road at least in the short term, but the loss of beach material from the foreshore could be aggravated. This process is thought to relate to the reduced capacity of hard sea defences to absorb wave energy (compared with natural shingle beaches) causing the returning backwash to scour sediment from the edge of the sea defence. (At Beesands in the 1980s, installation of rock rip-rap was followed by shingle scour and undermining of the rock boulders, leading to the eventual construction of a much more substantial rock, steel and concrete wall.) Sea defences would enable existing routeways to be maintained at least in the short term but might aggravate the problem of shingle loss, requiring much heavier defence works in the future. The landscape impact would be considerable as a previously natural soft shoreline would be converted to a hard managed boundary. A strip of sparsely vegetated pioneer vegetation habitat would be lost.

Abandoning the roadway would allow the shoreline to adjust naturally to the wave conditions, and

Factual enquiry	Route and key questions	Values enquiry
more objective data ← – –	– – – – – – – – – – –	– – → more subjective data
Sections of shoreline at Slapton appear to be eroding, threatening to wash away the main road and car parks.	**OBSERVATION AND PERCEPTION**	If beach levels are eroding, local opinions differ as to whether sea defences should be extended or not.
Is the Slapton beach system in an equilibrium or disequilibrium state? What are the implications for coastal management? Compare surveys and maps of past and present shorelines to determine stability. Surveys show seasonal equilibrium but long-term disequilibrium.	**DEFINITION AND DESCRIPTION** What? and Where?	Collect information about people's opinions (local residents, visitors and public bodies) concerning beach stability and what management they favour.
Surveys show seasonal equilibrium but long-term disequilibrium. Projected erosion rates indicate undermining of roadway in foreseeable future. Continued monitoring of beach profiles to assess rate of erosion.	**ANALYSIS AND EXPLANATION** How? and Why?	A high level of awareness of the problem was found but disagreement over management. Extension of sea defences, closure of road and re-alignment of road all proposed. Beach nourishment or waiting to see if beach re-forms naturally are other options.
Closing road would allow shoreline to readjust but would inconvenience local people. Extending sea defences could aggravate beach erosion. Re-alignment would encroach on nature reserve.	**PREDICTION AND EVALUATION** What might? What will? With what impact?	Public bodies with support of most local people favour more sea defences but strongly opposed by a minority of local people who either favour road closure or re-alignment.
Extension to sea defences or re-alignment of road seems the most likely option. Mobility of local people maintained but some nature reserve habitat loss. Sea defences may cause further beach erosion.	**DECISION-MAKING** What decision? With what impact?	Opposing voices likely to organise vigorous campaign to reverse decision.

PERSONAL EVALUATION AND JUDGEMENT
What do I think? Why?

Opposed to extension to sea defences on grounds of adverse impact on landscape and habitat and possilbility of aggravated beach erosion. Would accept re-alignment but favour road closure and restoration of natural shoreline.

PERSONAL RESPONSE
What next? What shall I do?

Continue current monitoring, disseminate findings and promote road closure policy through discussion and representation to public bodies.

Figure 5.10   The route to enquiry applied to the Slapton beach erosion issue.

44

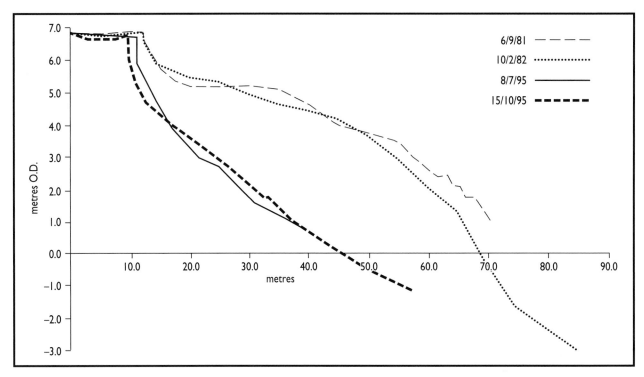

Figure 5.11   Beach erosion at Slapton, 1981–95.

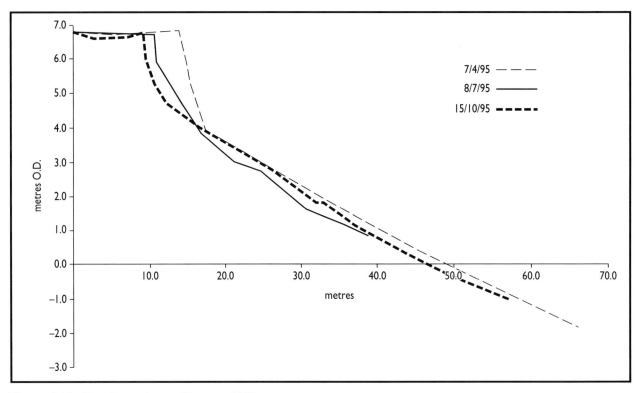

Figure 5.12   Beach erosion at Slapton, 1995.

removal of the tarmac would enable plant succession to re-establish vegetation cover and increase wild habitat. Journey times for local people would be increased with possible congestion on the alternative routes, many of which would use narrow lanes. This policy would also require far-reaching planning measures to achieve traffic reduction and alternative means of transport.

The policy of road re-alignment would involve encroaching on nature reserve land. The relocated road would run closer to the ley, causing greater disturbance to the nearby wetland habitat. While both sea defences and re-alignment would involve loss of habitat, the latter would involve loss of a larger area but the former would destroy a scarcer habitat supporting species with greater rarity.

Table 5.2   The main impacts of three alternative policies for action

Option	Main impacts
1. Hold the line • Build sea wall to defend existing road and car park.	Loss of shoreline habitat. Visual intrusion. Existing transport links and recreation provision maintained.
2. Divert • Shift road and car park landwards. Dig up and restore existing road and car park.	Shoreline habitats maintained. Local transport infrastructure maintained. Habitat loss to new road and car park.
3. Retreat • Abandon road and car park and allow shoreline to adjust.	Habitats maintained. Landscape and habitat gains as roadway and car park returned to nature. Reduced access to coast and nature reserve on central zone and reduced public pressure. Possible increase in pressure elsewhere.

Decision-making

The most likely outcome, based on past policy, is piecemeal extension of sea defences as threats to infrastructure occur. This would reflect the prevailing public view that roads and settlements ought to and can be defended against the sea but some individuals and public bodies would strongly oppose the visual and habitat disturbance to a largely natural stretch of coast in a National Nature Reserve. This outcome is understandable in the light of the priority which local people attach to mobility. If the road along the line were closed it would undoubtedly restrict the mobility of a significant number of people. While alternative main roads exist for travel between Dartmouth and Kingsbridge, travel from villages such as Slapton would require an initial 8 km journey along a narrow lane in order to reach the main road that gives access to Kingsbridge and Dartmouth. With the decline in village services and employment, a large proportion of villagers need to travel regularly to nearby towns.

Personal evaluation

This is the stage in an enquiry where you need to relate your own values and priorities to the issue concerned. Conflicts often develop between the decisions you might favour from a broad or long-term geographical understanding and the immediate needs of people directly affected by the decisions. In this case study, a geographical perspective would tend to favour closure of the road and allowing the shoreline to change in response to coastal processes. However, this would be very unpopular with many local people who would have to re-organise their lives and whose livelihoods might be threatened by such changes unless other policies were also adopted to limit the impact of reduced mobility. Fundamental and emotive questions are raised by issues such as this as to whether natural environments should be managed to accommodate human needs and expectations or whether those needs and expectations have to be modified to fit in with natural processes. In this example, if we adopt a decision based on somewhat idealistic geographical perspectives rather than practical short-term thinking, then we need to think carefully about how to explain a possibly unpopular policy to others and what broader planning decisions might be required to reduce the adverse effects of the chosen policy on some people's lives. Furthermore, in a democratic setting one should not seek to impose a policy that goes against a majority view. Personal action therefore needs to focus on convincing the majority of the wisdom of your decision.

You might be tempted to assist your decision-making by applying the technique of cost-benefit analysis (CBA), a method that has been applied elsewhere on this coast in order to justify the building of new sea walls. Using established cost-benefit methods, economists would identify the costs and benefits of each scenario and the decision would be taken on the project which had the highest ratio of benefit to cost. There are obvious difficulties here (as in many applications of CBA) in ascribing monetary values to fundamentally unquantifiable things such as rare species, habitat and landscape, though amazingly economists have attempted to do so. There have been some thoroughly discredited instances where sites of natural importance have been ascribed a monetary value of zero because it was argued they are protected, therefore the land is not available for commercial development and therefore in the free market has no monetary value. If CBA were applied to this case study it is likely that the high cost of building a sea wall would be offset against a higher cost of abandoning the road, the latter being based upon increased journey times and possible road widening elsewhere. Applying CBA to policy decisions tends to encourage reductionist planning by confining attention to a few quantifiable variables.

So, in summary, if you go for option 1 you would probably have the support of most (but not all) of the local community and of most people who use the road and live elsewhere, including the large number of holidaymakers who like to drive to the central car park. You would, though, upset a substantial number of nature lovers.

Option 2 would involve laying tarmac over a substantial area of nature reserve, but the existing road and car park could be restored to something approaching a natural habitat. You might find, though, that as the sea encroached further you would be faced in the future with the same problem all over again.

Option 3 would certainly get the votes of the majority of lovers of yellow-horned poppies but would require a lot of careful explanation to the local people. Unless you took trouble to explain the wider context of the plan, you might run considerable risk of being thrown into the sea. Future generations might erect a monument to you, though.

Personal action

Unlike this example, many issues are characterised by groups of local people opposing some environmental change which a public authority or commercial organisation is seeking to implement. In such cases, you might well decide to act with others through various forms of campaigning to oppose the change and reverse decisions. In this case study you might find yourself in a more isolated position with few allies. Your first actions would need to focus on convincing local people of your position, then to mobilise public opinion to influence public authorities. Such a stance requires courage and confidence that your chosen decision is the right one.

Extending your field investigations by participating in decision-making in this way offers opportunities for personal fulfilment, especially if you have visions and dreams of a better world. It could be counter-productive, though, to try to impose your visions on others, especially if you do not live in the place concerned. The role of the geographer here is perhaps to offer information about environmental change and to articulate future options, including those that draw on a holistic rather than a reductionist perspective. These are then available for the community to discuss, debate and ultimately use as a basis for decision-making. Further ideas about how field investigations can lead to action for change are presented in Chapter 6.

Conclusion

This summary of a case study of a fieldwork enquiry emphasises the conflicting viewpoints which are likely to occur at a time when major adjustments are taking place in how we view and interpret the world. In this example, the majority views appear to be based on established interpretations while the minority view is more closely linked to a more uncertain world view.

The differing perspectives might be summarised as in Table 5.3.

Many issues therefore may need to be seen in relation to a majority view which has yet to adjust to a number of newer interpretations of our relationship with the natural world.

Table 5.3   Summary of views

	Majority view	*Minority view*
The relationship between human expectations and natural processes	Nature can be adapted to satisfy human desires and expectations.	Human expectations may need to be reduced to accommodate natural processes.
Predictability of change	Scientific research can predict the outcome of different decisions.	Science can suggest possible outcomes of change but much environmental change is unpredictable.
Equilibrium	Systems tend towards equilibrium and return to previous states if disturbed.	Change is the norm and even landforms come and go.

Reflections

Thinking back to ideas in Chapter 2 about different views on environmental change and applying them to both the case studies in this chapter, we can perhaps see that according to how we select and interpret our field data and what time-scales we adopt we could use our findings to support more than one explanation of things. If we just compare the summer and winter profiles over a few years (as described elsewhere: Job, 1989) we would tend towards a neat static equilibrium model in which the build-up of the beach in summer alternated with lowering in winter, with negative feedback operating to keep the beach level within limits. Taking a longer view (the past fifteen years), there is evidence of declining beaches at Slapton over which the seasonal variations are superimposed, and this trend is evident over an even longer time-span at Beesands and Hallsands. Systems thinking would call this *dynamic equilibrium* – long-term change with short-term fluctuations superimposed. Taking an even longer view and drawing on map evidence from the early nineteenth century, we might deduce that the stock of shingle has generally been drifting north then south over the centuries with sometimes more at the north end of the bay and less at the south. In this model perhaps the storms of the early twentieth century just caught Hallsands with its shingle down (with a little help from the dredgers).

Or maybe the whole system has just reached the end of its life. It has only been there for 2,000 years, and nothing lasts for ever. Could it be that we just happen to be looking at the thing in its declining years?

We started these geographical explorations of Start Bay with a personal experience. What might we learn about ourselves from our investigations? Possibly that in the declining beach system we see mirrored our own mortality. Our response is to first say 'something must be wrong – there is change, not stability'. We intervene, to try and prolong; we must keep things the same, especially what we have built and find convenient, fooling ourselves all the while that this is possible while blaming ourselves (or others who have gone before us) for the demise of the thing in the first place.

We may also come to see that there is no such thing as hard science or objective data. Whatever information we gather is coloured and interpreted through a cultural and personal perspective.

Suggestions for further activities

- What links could be made between the Start Bay coast and global processes?

- Compare investigations 1 and 2 in this chapter. Which:
  a) tells us more about the processes at work on this coastline
  b) is of greater relevance
  c) gives a more holistic view of the coast
  d) establishes a stronger sense of place?

- To what extent was quantitative data important in each of the two approaches, or could similar conclusions have been reached from qualitative information alone?

6 Fieldwork towards a more sustainable world – investigations into action

- *What is meant by sustainability?*

- *How can fieldwork be organised so that it addresses sustainability issues?*

- *What examples are there of fieldwork in a context of sustainability issues?*

- *How can a fieldwork enquiry lead to change towards a more sustainable world?*

Introduction

Looking down from an upper floor flat onto the Great West Road as it disgorges the traffic from the M4 into central London, I begin to wonder about the origins, purposes and destinations of these seemingly urgent journeys. It is an almost continuous flow, day and night, which sustains a steady roar of rubber on tarmac. It has diversity – a mix of commuters' cars perhaps from rural haunts in Berkshire, taxis and minibuses bringing tourists and business people to and from the airport, trucks loaded with food, perhaps processed on the industrial estates of Middlesex or jetted in from tropical latitudes via Heathrow.

Such speculation is a reminder of how cities are linked not only to their regional setting but increasingly to distant places. In the short term such movements might be seen to sustain the city in economic terms but beyond the day-to-day financial transactions, what are the wider implications of this road? To the local community it is primarily a barrier. To get to the park and the riverside pubs on the other side of the road means negotiating stark and forbidding pedestrian subways. Its traffic emits oxides of nitrogen, carbon monoxide, hydrocarbons and small particles that penetrate the lungs, contributing to levels of pollution that frequently exceed recommended safe levels. It is also a massive converter of fossil carbon into atmospheric carbon dioxide. Paradoxically, it is part of a system that boosts economies while dividing and polluting the neighbourhood, and contributing to unpredictable changes in climate.

Traditionally, field investigations of an urban highway such as this might have focused on recording traffic flows, perhaps examining diurnal variations in types of traffic and directional flows.

Such investigations could so easily be taken a step further – to consider for example the daily emissions of carbon dioxide or particulates from one day's traffic or to explore how the road affects the lives and mobility of people in the immediate neighbourhood.

The purpose of this chapter is to consider how explorations and investigations of local environments through fieldwork might help us to take a fresh look at how things are as a starting point to new ways of interpreting our surroundings and perhaps changing them for the better.

Local Agenda 21 – a context for fieldwork towards sustainability

It seems a fair time since the world's nations gathered in Rio in 1992 for the United Nations Conference on Environment and Development (UNCED), often referred to as the Rio Earth Summit. Three important statements of intent emerged from the event which together have the potential to create a healthier, more egalitarian and more sustainable planet. These were the Biodiversity Convention, the Framework Climate Change Convention, and Agenda 21. All are highly relevant to geography but Agenda 21 has particular importance to us if we are interested in investigating our local environment with a view to changing it in ways that create improvements in quality of life locally as well as contributing in small ways to tackling global problems.

The Agenda 21 statements make up a weighty and wordy document but their essence can be summed up as a programme for working towards 'sustainable development'. There are numerous interpretations of sustainable development but the principle of meeting people's needs and improving quality of life without damaging present or future environments or depleting finite resources is one that can be applied to both the developed and less developed worlds. It is easy to criticise the concept of sustainability – the term is sometimes applied inappropriately as well as being one of the rather overused words of the nineties. Its widespread application to the city context is often seen as impossibly idealistic. Cities, it is argued, will always consume more energy and resources than they produce, so how can they ever be sustainable? It is more useful perhaps to think in terms of moving towards greater sustainability rather than trying to devise city systems which are totally self-sufficient in energy and resource terms.

Over two-thirds of the statements in Agenda 21 are thought to require the co-operation and commitment of local government and local communities, hence the relevance to local fieldwork projects. Chapter 28 calls on all local authorities to develop local strategies towards sustainability. More importantly, the ideas for change are intended to spring from the needs and aspirations of local communities – that is you, me, the people next door, the homeless, old and young and all cultural and ethnic groups – a fairly diverse bunch of people, each with their own needs and aspirations.

Unsurprisingly, true community participation in the local implementation of Agenda 21 is proving hard to achieve. It is one of many initiatives which, while promoting 'bottom-up' community-based decision-making, has originated from a 'top down' process set in motion by international governments. Many people will never have heard of it and those who have often perceive it as being a global environmental agenda rather than a programme that aims to fuse together environmental, poverty and quality of life issues largely through planning and change in the local environment. Others see it as creating an illusion of people power, arguing that it might give people the feeling of having some influence over their local circumstances and environment while the real power is still retained by big companies and remote centralised governments. A further obstacle is that those with the worst quality of life, the marginalised, dispossessed or disaffected members of society, are unlikely to see their problems in global environmental terms and often feel marginalised and excluded from the established processes of decision-making.

As geographers, our training should help us to make the vital connections between local and global issues as well as enabling us to see what reallocation of resources and power will be needed to improve the quality of life for everyone, especially the poor and powerless. The case studies in this chapter offer examples of fieldwork investigations in the context of the intentions of local Agenda 21 and sustainability issues.

Indicators of sustainabilty

Before we can consider particular environments that we might investigate in the field which relate to the issues of sustainability, we need to have some idea in our minds of how we might assess degrees of sustainability. Each book, article or conference on the subject seems to come up with its own definition, which can become confusing. Inevitably, the sort of emphasis you give to the idea of sustainability depends upon your values and beliefs (see Chapter 2). The more popular definitions put *people* at the centre of the definition, arguing that sustainability means using the Earth's resources in ways that improve the quality of life for all, while not depleting resources or disrupting the natural processes upon which we depend through pollution. Mention is usually made of future generations, arguing that our present lifestyles should not compromise the rights of future generations to have access to basic resources, beautiful landscapes and unpolluted land, water and air.

Such criteria might be described as reflecting an *anthropocentric* viewpoint – one that puts people at the centre of things and regards resources, landscapes and other life forms as having a value mainly in relation to human needs and aspirations. Deeper green ideas might prefer a definition of sustainability that recognises the equal rights of all life forms to flourish undisturbed and unharmed. Human activity, it would be argued, should therefore aim to minimise disturbance of the natural world through simple living, consuming less and replacing the use of finite resources with renewables. Others take a more social or political stance, arguing that while inequalities persist there will always be deprivation, instability and violence which ultimately threaten the security of people and the ecosystems upon which they depend.

It is sometimes argued that it doesn't matter too much what you mean by sustainable development provided you get on with it, though this assumes that there is sufficient common ground among the different viewpoints to allow some sort of consensus to be reached. Rather than seeking single definitions of sustainability, many people who are interested in change towards a more sustainable world refer to *indicators* of sustainability. These are fairly specific criteria against which an activity, an environment or a community might be assessed in order to judge how closely it meets sustainable objectives. A number of suggested criteria are listed below.

Some suggested indicators of sustainability

1. *The degree to which resource use is linear or cyclical*
   Are materials or energy being used so that waste is minimised by re-use, recycling or the use of renewable sources?

2. *The degree to which human interaction is fragmentary or convivial*
   Do people meet in the course of their daily lives in a way that encourages them to undertake joint tasks or offer mutual support? Are people interacting in a friendly, relaxed way or does the environment they're in make people feel stressed, tense, threatened, aggressive or isolated?

3. *The extent to which production and consumption are international, national or local*
   Are the goods and services people use coming from within the local area and community? If so, the need for energy, materials, packaging and transportation will be decreased. (This criterion need not apply to information technology.)

4. *The degree to which the control of an activity is outside the control of local people or is excercised democratically by them*
   The more people control or influence the production of energy, goods and services, the more likely they are to be able to minimise pollution and environmental damage. (A key feature of sustainable development under Agenda 21 is the involvement of previously disadvantaged groups in the decision-making process.)

5. *The extent to which an activity diminishes the ecological base or promotes biodiversity*
   The more an activity reduces or simplifies a habitat, e.g. through monoculture, the more likely it is that biodiversity will be decreased. It has been suggested that activities which meet criteria 1–4 will also tend to promote biodiversity.

Some of these criteria may surprise you as they are not just about ecosystems, conservation and resources. The Agenda includes social concerns and the extent to which communities are self-reliant, and decision-making is decentralised. The thinking here is that local communities are more likely to show care and concern for their surroundings than remote bureaucracies or large profit-driven corporations. This is one set of indicators for assessing the extent to which an activity achieves sustainable goals. There are many other possible criteria depending upon your own interpretation of the concept. One of the activities at the end of this chapter suggests how you might go about establishing your own list of indicators.

Getting started in the urban environment

Sustainability issues are just as relevant to the rural as to the urban environment, though the case studies in this chapter focus on the urban setting. The concept can be applied as readily to farms and villages as to cities, factories and transport systems. This section focuses on beginning an investigation with a sustainability theme in the urban setting.

For city dwellers, the built environment is so familiar that it is possible to walk through it without noticing very much. We often pass through wrapped up in our own thoughts, avoiding eye contact with passers-by for fear of antagonising somebody. We are if anything overloaded with stimuli and rapidly changing images. Cutting off and withdrawing become survival mechanisms. This response is unhelpful, though, if we are setting out on a process of investigation or enquiry where we need to maximise our awareness of what's going on around us and, more importantly, ask critical questions about what is taking place, and see some of the less obvious meanings behind our observations. The traffic jam belching fumes into the city air, the homeless person asleep in the shop doorway, the row of empty houses with boarded-up windows, the bleakness of the pedestrian subway – they all have causes, consequences and, if we think a little deeper, perhaps connections as well.

There are several ways of focusing our senses so that we not only observe more but also think more deeply about what we observe. Just walking around an area with no pre-planned route in mind encourages us to notice things. We begin to make decisions about which route to take based on choices: Which places look interesting and attract us? Which do we choose to avoid because they seem uninteresting or threatening? Taking a camera, notebook or sketchbook provides further reason to focus on particular features in the urban environment in that we make more specific choices about what we find interesting, beautiful, amusing or disturbing – and therefore worthy of recording. Such simple activities in themselves may be all that's needed to set us going on the first stage of the fieldwork strategy outlined in Figure 3.7. This strategy begins with activities to heighten awareness based on personal experience of an environment, a process sometimes described as *acclimatisation* as described on page 23.

This chapter attempts to set urban fieldwork investigations in the more specific context of sustainability issues. How can we begin to judge whether an environment as complex and difficult to understand as a city meets criteria for sustainable development? For this purpose you may find the stimulus cards in Figure 6.1 helpful. These describe short activities that you can undertake at intervals as you explore an area, each focusing attention on some aspect of the environment, most of which relate in some way to sustainability issues. An element of randomness can be introduced by transferring the tasks to cards, shuffling the cards, setting off on foot then stopping at timed intervals and carrying out the activity on the top card. Rather than using the stimulus cards offered here, an alternative would be to write your own set based on your personal ideas about sustainability issues as described at the end of this chapter.

As in Chapter 5, having experienced an environment in an open-ended way it is useful to withdraw and pause for reflection before focusing on a more specific investigation. An acclimatisation experience normally throws up a whole mixture of events, observations and feelings which could lead to many possible investigations. Here is a summary of some experiences remembered by students after exploring an inner city area of West London, partly with the help of stimulus cards:

> Contrasting living conditions – bleak tower blocks by the flyover and big Georgian houses overlooking the river.
> A disturbed street dweller busily gathering discarded fruit from the market dump.
> A recently restored Victorian suspension bridge over the river.

> Litter-strewn pavements outside the riverside pubs.
> Angry drivers on the slip-road to the flyover.
> Conversations interrupted by traffic noise.
> Feeling scared in the pedestrian subway.
> Long waits to cross the road.
> Multicoloured houseboats on the river.
> Smoky fumes from buses in the traffic jam.
> The banter of the market traders.
> The bland and sterile shopping mall.
> The number of sandwich shops.
> Gordon's secondhand bike stall.
> Coca-Cola's shiny new office building.
> Children playing in the street (but not in the park).

Clearly there was no shortage of memorable events – some pleasant, some disturbing, others invoking no particular emotion – but most were memorable because they involved feelings and emotion.

Having derived a random collection of remembered events such as this, it is not difficult to begin to pick out themes and, from these, begin to formulate key questions and then project titles. Table 6.1 provides a list of key questions and associated project titles which arose from random observations during the exploration of the inner city.

These key questions (and the memorable experiences which gave rise to them) may not be the sorts of questions which occur to geographers brought up only on a diet of models and hypothesis testing. They are, though, the sorts of questions which one begins to ask when you start to view the world from a critical viewpoint peppered with some basic geographical understanding together with some personal concept of what sustainable development might be about.

The following examples, drawn mainly from local fieldwork examples in the city environment, show how practical studies can be linked to the broader theme of sustainability. They focus in turn on the linked themes of air quality and transportation, and include a mixture of both quantitative and more qualitative methods.

Investigating air quality

Even without using quantitative methods, our own experiences of urban streets, observing or talking to other people, and reading or hearing press reports, make us aware of air pollution as an issue. We have surely all held our breath in a traffic-filled

52

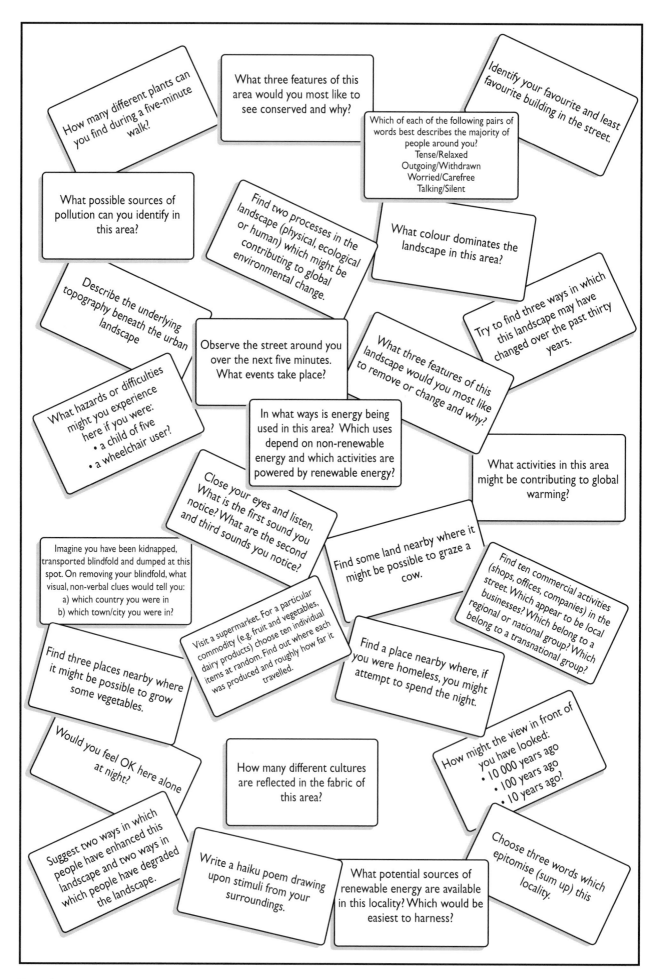

Figure 6.1   Stimulus cards for an urban environment.

Table 6.1   Key questions and associated project titles arising from random observations of the inner city

Key question	Project title
How much packaging, transportation and energy are used by market stalls compared with supermarkets?	A comparison of resource and energy consumption between market stalls and a supermarket
How far do street dwellers travel during their daily activities?	The territory and sphere of activity of street dwellers
How do exhaust emissions from public transport compare with those from private transport?	Public perception and field measurement of exhaust emissions from public and private transport
How much carbon dioxide is emitted in a day on the Great West Road?	An evaluation of the contribution of the Great West Road to climate change
Does air quality in the locality meet international standards?	A quantitative assessment of urban air quality in relation to international limits and guidelines
What happens to used bottles and cans discarded by the riverside?	The actual and potential level of glass and can recycling in the neighbourhood
What happens to discarded fruit and vegetables from the market?	The potential development of an urban community composting scheme
Do the new office developments help or hinder the lives of the less well-off?	The impact of new office development on the poorest people in the community
Who buys Gordon's old bikes and where do they come from?	The social and ecological significance of a secondhand bike stall
Is there a conflict between the new Tesco store and the borough's policy of traffic reduction?	The effects of a new urban superstore on traffic and air pollution

street to avoid inhaling a particularly noxious lungful of exhaust fumes. How many urban cyclists are wearing face masks to attempt to protect themselves from vehicle emissions? Such experiences open up a range of key questions which could form starting points for air quality investigations. These might include:

Does air quality in a locality meet safe standards?
How does air quality vary in areas with different amounts of traffic?
How does air quality vary between narrow streets and broad streets?
How does air quality vary with changing weather conditions?
How does air quality vary from the city centre to the surrounding countryside?
Does the day-to-day experience of sensitive people (e.g. people with respiratory difficulties) relate to varying air quality?
Do daily hospital admissions for respiratory

complaints relate to varying air quality?
How significant is air pollution in people's concerns, compared with other urban problems?

Answering some of these questions may require largely quantitative investigation but qualitative information would be equally valid in other cases.

Air pollution issues are central to many ideas about sustainability. At one level, poor air quality may have very direct effects on human health. At another level, some aspects of air pollution (e.g. carbon dioxide and methane emissions) have close links with the issues of climate change and global warming. Studies focusing on air quality have relevance at a range of scales. Air pollution may have direct adverse effects on the health of people living in the neighbourhood, particularly children, the elderly and people with heart or lung problems. Pollution generated locally may have far-reaching impacts regionally and globally. Ground-level ozone, for example, forms from vehicle emissions reacting with sunlight which then drifts on the wind to give high concentrations elsewhere, often in rural areas far from the sources of pollution. Oxides of sulphur and nitrogen contribute to acid rain which may fall on areas remote from where pollutants are generated. Even if pollutants such as oxides of nitrogen and sulphur are removed from emissions by converters and scrubbers, any process that involves the combustion of fossil fuels will release extra carbon dioxide into the atmosphere. Although there are more potent greenhouse gases than carbon dioxide which are released into the atmosphere, its significance lies in the sheer scale of fossil fuel combustion on Earth, currently running at 8.5 million tonnes per day from combustion of oil products alone. Although conclusive proof linking air pollution with a range of health problems and environmental issues is sometimes hard to establish, there is abundant cause for concern that air pollution (increasingly from motor traffic) is having harmful effects on people, the atmosphere and the climate.

Some air pollution issues

The topic can seem a little daunting as the term 'air pollution' covers a wide range of individual pollutants, each of which has specific sources, particular effects on health and various effects on the wider environment including the atmosphere and climate. Table 6.2 attempts to summarise the main atmospheric pollutants about which there is concern, and their probable impacts on health and the environment.

If you are investigating particular pollutants it would be helpful to carry out further reading on what is known about their impact (see Read, 1994). When researching the effects of particular pollutants the following questions might be used as a guide to such research:

1. Is it thought to be directly harmful to metabolic processes in people, animals and/or plants (e.g. carbon monoxide)? In the case of human health, is it thought to be linked to respiratory problems, is it carcinogenic or linked to other health problems?

2. Is it a greenhouse gas which contributes to the absorption of outgoing longwave radiation, thereby promoting global warming (e.g. CO_2 and CH_4)?

3. Is it an 'acid' gas which could contribute to acid rain or dry acid deposition (e.g. NO_2 and SO_2)?

4. Is it an ozone-destroying gas which contributes to ozone depletion in the upper atmosphere (e.g. CFCs)?

(Individual pollutants may well have an impact under more than one of these categories.)

While different pollutants have different sources (Table 6.2), motorised traffic burning fossil fuels can be identified as a major source of most but not all of the pollutants. Figure 6.2 shows the sources of NO_2 pollution during the 1980s and the growing contribution from road transport.

Despite awareness of the harm done by pollutants emitted by motor traffic, most economic and social trends are still tending to increase emissions. Although devices such as catalytic converters and more efficient fuel use can cut emissions from individual vehicles, these developments are generally more than offset by increased vehicle numbers. Increased levels of vehicle use in the developed world together with the rapid motorisation of transport in much of the less developed world is exacerbating most forms of air pollution at a global scale. The continuing expansion of the global economy combined with mass tourism, the spread of car culture, out-of-town shopping and ever longer commuting distances means that more journeys are being made to move around more goods and more people over greater distances. These are the sorts of broader issues which you might wish to refer to in your concluding material when writing up.

Planning an air pollution enquiry

An initial stage might involve identification of a critical key question based on your own experiences, talking to people in your neighbourhood about air quality, reading and critical thinking. There are a number of sources available which may be helpful in getting to grips with some of the technical issues involved in air pollution (Job, 1994a; Kirby, 1995; Read, 1994; Royal Commission on Environmental Pollution, 1994). Depending upon the nature of your key question there are a number of planning decisions to be made.

• Is the emphasis of the study spatial, temporal or both?

Table 6.2   Sources and effects of atmospheric pollutants

Pollutant	Main source	Health effect	Environmental effect
Nitrogen dioxide (NO_2)	One of the oxides of nitrogen emitted in vehicle exhausts.	May exacerbate asthma and increase lung infections.	Contributes to acid rain.
Sulphur dioxide (SO_2)	Mainly produced by coal burning. Some emitted by diesel vehicles.	Exacerbates asthma and causes wheezing and chronic bronchitis.	Contributes to acid rain.
Particulates (PM10s) Total suspended particulates Black smoke	Includes a wide range of solid and liquid particles. The smallest (<10 microns) penetrate deep into the lungs. Diesel vehicles produce more than petrol engines.	Linked with a wide range of respiratory and heart diseases. Particulates can carry carcinogenic compounds deep into the lungs.	Blackens buildings and street furniture. Coats vegetation and affects plant metabolism
Carbon monoxide (CO)	Mainly from petrol engines.	Reduces the ability of the blood to carry oxygen by combining with haemoglobin. Fatal at high doses. At low doses exacerbates heart disease, can harm the foetus and impairs concentration and nerve function.	
Ozone (O_3)	Forms in warm sunny weather from the interaction of oxides of nitrogen with VOCs. Although the ingredients are traffic–derived, concentrations are often highest in rural areas. High levels may develop far from the source of the ingredients.	Irritates eyes and respiratory system. Exacerbates asthma. Causes rapid deterioration of rubber products.	Adversely affects plant growth.
Lead	Present in leaded petrol.	Harms brain development in children.	Accumulates in crops and soil.
Volatile organic compounds (VOCs)	A group of organic compounds emitted from the evaporation of solvents and petrol. Also present in exhaust fumes.	Carcinogenic (cancer-inducing).	
Polycyclic aromatic hydrocarbons (PAHs)	Produced by incomplete combustion of fuel. Become attached to particulates.	Carcinogenic.	
Methane (CH_4)	Produced from anaerobic decomposition of organic matter in landfill sites and intensive livestock farming.	Not toxic at atmospheric concentrations. Can build up to cause explosions on old landfill sites.	A powerful greenhouse gas and involved in stratospheric ozone depletion.
Carbon dioxide (CO_2)	Produced from any combustion of carbon-based fuel (oil, coal, wood) and aerobic decomposition of organic matter. Deforestation increases CO_2 by decreasing carbon uptake by photosynthesis.	Not toxic at atmospheric concentrations.	A greenhouse gas, contributing to global warming.
Chlorofluorocarbons (CFCs)	Synthesised compounds widely used in the 1980s in refrigeration, as an aerosol propellant and in foam-blown packaging. Manufacture of CFCs is being phased out but large quantities are still in circulation.	Not toxic at atmospheric concentrations.	Destroys stratospheric ozone increasing the risk of cataracts, skin cancers and sunburn. Also a greenhouse gas.

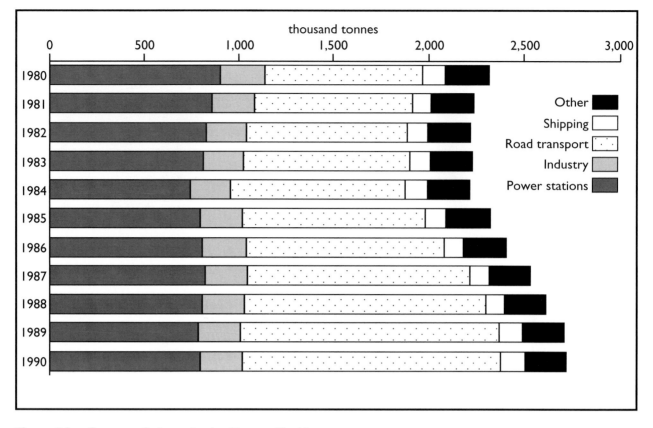

Figure 6.2   Sources of atmospheric nitrogen dioxide.

Air quality and its effects, in common with many other phenomena, often show large and interesting variations from place to place (spatial variation) and over time (temporal variation). Spatial variation may be associated with different levels of emissions (e.g. a busy roadside compared with a residential street or park) and the ease with which polluted air is dispersed or contained (e.g. a narrow street confined between tall buildings compared with an open roadside away from buildings). Variation at a site over short periods of time (e.g. diurnal variation) often relates to changing amounts of traffic, while variations over a series of days might be investigated in relation to weather changes.

- Is the study going to be based on qualitative information or quantitative data or both?

Most investigations would normally include some quantitative data – that is, information usually in a numeric form about variables which can be measured. Do not, however, undervalue qualitative data – that is, descriptions of events, people's accounts of how they feel and your own sensory experience. Such information is at least as real and significant as numbers on a meter or in a spreadsheet. There are abundant opportunities with air pollution investigations for combining the two

forms of data. For example, you might either collect yourself or obtain from official monitoring stations, daily readings of air quality variables such as nitrogen dioxide or carbon monoxide. You could also ask a group of asthma sufferers to keep diaries of their health and perceptions of air quality, then examine the two sets of information in relation to each other.

- Is it to be mainly concerned with causes, effects or both?

In Figure 6.3 each of the boxes can be regarded as either a cause or an effect and in some cases both. Any arrow in the diagram that links two boxes is suggesting a relationship between two factors. Thus the amount and type of emissions at the site (the cause) are thought to affect the type and concentration of pollutants (the effect). When we go on to consider the consequences of the pollu-tants then the pollutant concentration becomes the cause and the boxes below become the effects. When plotting graphs of one variable against another it is important to know which variable is which. The variable which is the effect (the dependent variable) is plotted on the y (vertical) axis and the cause (independent variable) goes on the x (horizontal) axis. So if you were plotting traffic counts against some measure of air quality

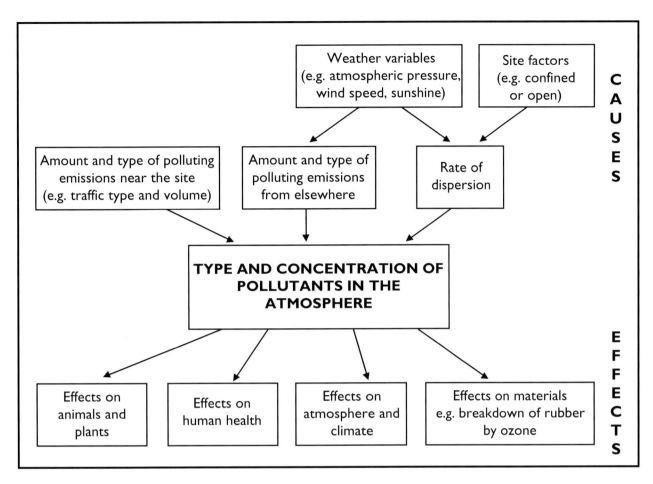

Figure 6.3   A framework for investigating air quality.

such as carbon monoxide (CO) concentration then traffic would go on the horizontal axis and CO on the vertical axis. If though you were plotting NO_2 against hospital admissions for asthma, NO_2 would be the independent variable and hospital admissions the dependent variable.

The terms 'dependent and independent' and indeed 'cause and effect' can be misleading if you are thinking holistically, as variables can be both causes and effects in a web of interlinkages. The problem with two-dimensional graphs and simple bivariate correlation is that such methods of analysis can only cope with a single relationship between two variables. That's all right provided you remember that you are only looking at one link in a web of interrelationships.

•   What information will be derived from secondary sources and what information from primary data?

Most personal investigations will be required to include some primary data – that is, data you have collected yourself from your own observations or measurements. There is no harm in combining

primary and secondary data. For example, you might collect your own information about pollution levels and traffic volume then use weather data from the Meteorological Office or elsewhere to analyse the air pollution data. Alternatively, you could obtain air pollution data from the Department of Environment monitoring stations and compare this with your own weather data. If you are able to obtain health statistics such as daily admissions of asthma cases at a nearby hospital, this would be a very valuable secondary data source.

Units and standards

If you are collecting your own primary data on air quality or referring to secondary data, you will need to be familiar with the units that are used for measuring concentrations of pollutants and the standards which have been set specifying supposedly 'safe' or acceptable concentrations of pollutants.

The units for measuring pollutants are either expressed as the weight of pollutant per volume of air or the volume of pollutant in a given volume of air. In the case of the former you will come across units given in either μg/m³ (micrograms per cubic metre, i.e. millionths of grams per cubic metre) or mg/m³ (milligrams per cubic metre, i.e. thousandths of grams per cubic metre). For solid particulates, concentrations are always expressed in this form but for gaseous pollutants, concentrations are often converted to the volume-to-volume unit. This will be expressed as either parts per million (ppm) or parts per billion (ppb). In the field situation most pollutants occur at concentrations in the ppb range except for carbon monoxide which is frequently present in streets at concentrations within the ppm range.

Air quality standards are critical concentration levels defined by national governments or international bodies. These may be 'limits' which are legally enforceable or 'guides' which are targets or recommendations. A difficulty with both limits and guides is that they are generally designated in relation to human health, but there is no proven evidence for 'safe' levels, particularly as individuals show a tremendous variation in their reaction to pollutants. A further difficulty is that

standards designated as safe in relation to human health may not necessarily be safe for other life forms or in terms of broader environmental impact.

Some of the currently applied limits and guidelines are provided in Table 6.3.

The often confusing and conflicting detail of air quality standards perhaps illustrates the constraints of applying rigorous quantitative treatment to a complex environmental issue where causes and effects are imperfectly understood. Furthermore, generalised limits and guides which fail to take account of large differences between individuals in their tolerance of poor air quality may not be helpful. Are air pollution standards an area of environmental concern where we need to recognise the limitations of scientific understanding or are they better than nothing as a tool to achieving improved air quality? Our intuitive and perceived sense of air quality may be equally valid though assessments based on these qualitative criteria may be rejected by decision-makers who only deal in science-based knowledge. If we do recognise the limitations of science in this area, this gives added legitimacy to the more qualitative sorts of data you

Table 6.3   World Health Organisation (WHO) and European Union (EU) limits and guidelines on air quality

Nitrogen dioxide – standards and guidelines
The European Union Directive on standards for NO_2 are based on an analysis of mean hourly concentrations over a year. The limit of 104.6 ppb and the guide of 70.6 ppb refer to the 98th percentile of a year-long run of hourly values. If all the hourly values of NO_2 concentration were placed in ascending order then the value that includes 98% of all the data (but excludes the highest 2% of values) should not exceed 105 ppb. As a target for air quality improvement, the 98th percentile should not exceed 71 ppb. Research has shown that the long-term mean values obtained by exposing weekly samplers over several months (ideally a year) can be equated with the 98th percentile value. In several studies it has been shown that a simple multiplication of the long-term mean NO_2 concentration by a factor of 2.5 gives a good approximation of the 98th percentile value for that site.

Carbon monoxide: World Health Organisation guidelines

Mean concentration/duration	*Guide value (ppm)*
15-minute mean	87
30-minute mean	50
1-hour mean	30
8-hour mean	10

Sulphur dioxide: EU Directive limit and guide values

Reference period	*SO_2 concentration*	*Particulate concentration*
Limit value:	250 μg/m³ applies if:	>128 μg/m³
98th percentile of daily values	350 μg/m³ applies if:	<128 μg/m³
Guide value: 24-hour mean	100–150 μg/m³	
One-year mean	40–60 μg/m³	

may collect on the responses of people and plant growth to air quality. Such biological indicators may be the best guides to the health or otherwise of the atmosphere. The appearance of leafy lichens in city parks and squares rather than spreadsheets of data from computerised monitoring stations may be the best indicator that healthy air quality has been achieved.

Secondary data sources

Several of the important pollutants listed in Table 6.2 can only be measured using expensive and sophisticated equipment. These methods usually depend on some sort of infra-red absorption technique or an electrochemical sensor. Infra-red techniques depend upon the tendency for particular gases to absorb a specific wavelength within the infra-red radiation band. An emitter produces radiation at the specific wavelength which passes through a sample of atmosphere and then a receiver records how much radiation is received. The difference between emitted and received radiation will indicate the concentration of the gas in the atmosphere. This sort of equipment is operated at a national network of stations operated by the Department of the Environment and daily data can be obtained on a freephone number (0800 556677) or the air quality website (see page 64 for details of this site).

An example of this sort of secondary data is listed in Table 6.4. The first column of figures for each pollutant was recorded towards the end of a long warm spell with high atmospheric pressure and very low wind speeds over most of the country, while the July data are typical of a more westerly airstream with higher pressure gradients and windspeeds, dispersing pollutants from their mainly urban sources.

Nitrogen dioxide has aroused a lot of recent attention as it is thought to be not only a health hazard at high concentrations but also a major contribution to acid rain. Data for 10th June 1993 shows a typical pattern under conditions of high pressure and low wind speeds, with high concentrations for London (138 ppb for kerbside measurements) falling rapidly to 11 ppb in the rural south-east and 3 ppb in northern Scotland.

A major cause of the high urban concentrations is evident from Figure 6.2 showing detailed breakdowns of sources of NO_2 emissions for the UK in 1980–90. By 1990 road transport accounted

for 52 per cent of emissions with power stations contributing a further 28 per cent and industry 8 per cent (figures obtained from the National Atmospheric Emissions Inventory).

Supplementary data to help explain the differences between the two data sets might include weather

Table 6.4   Secondary air quality data

Nitrogen dioxide concentrations (ppb)

	10/6/93	9/7/93
Edinburgh	51	30
Glasgow	65	8
Belfast	73	27
Teesside	28	22
Leeds	62	27
Manchester	67	24
West Midlands	32	30
Birmingham	76	17
London Bloomsbury	122	41
London Victoria	109	35
London kerbside	138	42
London Earls Court	120	30
Cardiff	30	26
Merseyside	90	26
Bristol	65	23
Newcastle	62	39
Derbyshire	29	7
South-east England	11	1
Hertfordshire	31	5
North Scotland	3	0

Sulphur dioxide concentrations (ppb)

	10/6/93	9/7/93
Edinburgh	7	9
Sunderland	4	3
Belfast	109	13
Birmingham	19	7
Leeds	27	32
South Yorkshire	2	5
Hertfordshire	12	15
London Bloomsbury	41	9
London Victoria	53	8
London kerbside	36	15
Cardiff	16	3
Merseyside	78	4
Newcastle	8	8
Bristol	14	16
North Scotland	4	0
Derbyshire	25	12
South-east England	7	4

Table 6.4 (continued)   Secondary air quality data

Ozone concentrations (ppb)		
	10/6/93	*9/7/93*
Edinburgh	43	18
Belfast	44	32
Leeds	75	21
Birmingham	52	22
Hertfordshire	122	23
London Bloomsbury	73	14
London Victoria	62	23
Cardiff	84	15
Merseyside	37	26
Bristol	53	18
Newcastle	52	25
South-east England	110	42
Mid Scotland	57	36
South Scotland	109	33
Cumbria	106	26
North Ireland	50	33
North Yorkshire	99	31
Cheshire	58	19
Derbyshire	95	50
Nottinghamshire	61	14
Mid Wales	71	15
East Anglia	82	32
Oxfordshire	85	33
South East	110	33
South West	87	27

charts showing isobars, pressure systems and wind direction as well as weather data from a nearby meteorological station.

In order to analyse spatial patterns, plotting the data on an outline map of the UK may be helpful. Drawing in isolines can make the picture clearer but note that the sampling sites are not evenly distributed across the country and have been deliberately located to provide more data for urban areas. Consequently, rural areas are under-represented.

There is considerable controversy over the siting of some of the DoE monitoring stations, particularly concerning their representativeness of much of the air that people actually breathe in city streets.

Field methods for air quality assessment

While there is a growing range of instruments available for air pollution monitoring, many of these are not suitable for field monitoring or are prohibitively expensive. Many of the meters produced for measuring concentrations of airborne pollutants are designed for recording high concentrations only (normally in the parts per million range – ppm). These are for applications in industry to detect toxic levels in confined areas. With the exception of carbon monoxide which occurs at levels within the ppm range in street situations, most gaseous forms of air pollution are only detectable outdoors within the parts per billion (ppb) range. The methods described here have been selected on the basis of being:

- sensitive enough to give meaningful results at the concentrations occurring in the field

- affordable either for your own project or by a school or college department

- reasonably simple to use.

Nitrogen dioxide

Nitrogen dioxide digital meters are available to monitor NO_2, though at present portable and affordable instruments are insufficiently sensitive to record in the ppb range. However, methods using passive samplers have been developed. These are devices containing reagents which absorb NO_2 over a period of time. After a known period of exposure the samplers are sealed and returned for laboratory analysis to determine the amount of NO_2 absorbed which can then be related to the concentration of NO_2 in the atmosphere during the period of exposure. It needs to be borne in mind that such samplers will aggregate what are normally varying concentrations over the period of exposure. If left out for a week, for example, there may be peaks in concentration, which will elevate the aggregate value for that week, but won't record the value of the peak concentration. The value obtained is comparable to a mean value over the time of exposure. One such method has been developed by Dr Darius Krochmal at the University of Krakow in Poland. If you are studying chemistry and have use of a reasonably equipped chemistry laboratory with a spectrophotometer you could carry out your own analyses using Dr Krochmal's design of sampler and analytical methods. Alternatively, these samplers can be obtained from Krakow and returned there for analysis at reasonable rates. Comparable but more costly samplers called diffusion tubes together with an analysis service is also available in the UK from AEA Technology. (See page 64 for contact details.)

An example of a study using Dr Krochmal's samplers is the Schools Network on Air Pollution (SNAP) project, a study of London's air quality carried out in 1995. At each school two NO_2 samplers were exposed each week during the study, one in the school grounds to give a background reading and the other adjacent to a busy main road near the school. Figure 6.4 shows the results of mean weekly concentrations at a range of schools and other comparative locations during the summer of 1995. A clear pattern is evident, with rural sites away from London recording low values and urban sites showing increasing concentrations towards central London. If you locate your samplers close to main roads then you will probably find much higher values. Figure 6.5 shows the results from main roads located close to a sample of London schools, supplemented by a sample of roadside sites in Central London.

These examples are looking at spatial variation in air quality using mean values over a period of time. An alternative way of looking at these sorts of data is to consider a single site and look at variation over time which may relate to variations in traffic emissions or weather factors or both.

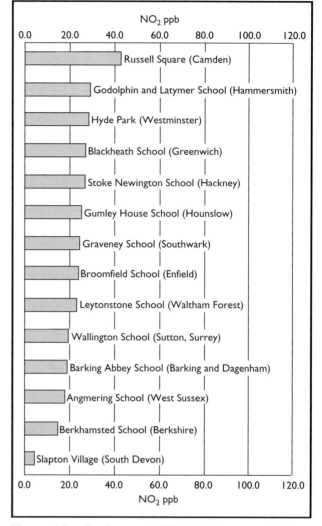

Figure 6.4   Background NO_2 data from passive samplers.

Carbon monoxide

Because carbon monoxide occurs at quite high concentrations in streets close to traffic, readings are detectable using digital meters which record within the ppm range. Though not cheap, such instruments may be affordable by a school or college geography department. CO meters are easy to use to give a digital readout of CO concentration in ppm in the field and can also be used to measure the CO content of a person's exhaled breath. The latter use is normally undertaken as part of health education programmes to discourage smoking, as there is a close correlation between smoking habits, CO in the blood and CO in exhaled breath. In terms of purchasing a CO meter, a possibility might be a joint purchase involving budgets from geography, science and health education. In the context of air quality monitoring, CO meters can be used in a variety of ways.

One possibility is to use it in the exhaled breath mode and record the CO concentration in the exhaled breath of non-smokers who have been in different air quality environments. You could try measuring CO in your own breath at intervals after exposure to different environments, for example before and after exposure to traffic in the street. Interesting comparisons can be drawn between exposure as a pedestrian, exposure during a cycle journey and exposure during a car or bus journey. If you know people who spend long periods of time close to dense traffic, such as cycle couriers, taxi drivers, road workers, homeless people or police personnel, you could try measuring their exhaled breath CO concentration against a sample of people who haven't been exposed to traffic. It would be necessary to ensure that they were non-smokers, otherwise their exposure to tobacco smoke would become the dominant factor. When interpreting the data you will need to consider that some of the variation between people will be due to physiological differences in their tendency to absorb and retain inhaled CO.

Other possibilities could involve using the meter to record variations in CO concentrations in streets with different traffic volumes. In order to ensure

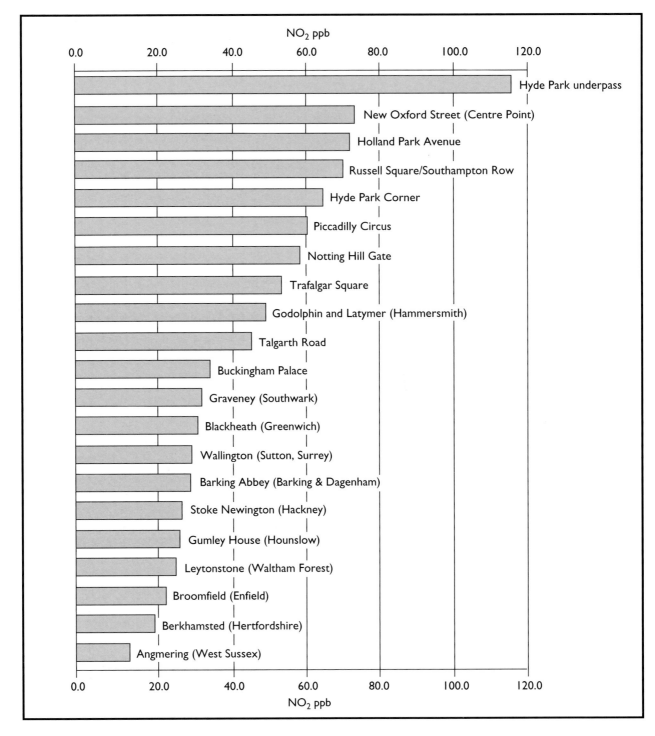

Figure 6.5   Roadside NO$_2$ data from passive samplers.

comparability between sites you will need to standardise the technique. In the Schools Network on Air Pollution project, the following standardised method was used.

- Stand at kerbside but out of danger from passing vehicles and hold meter 1.5 m above ground level with sampling port facing out into the street.

- Record CO reading every 15 seconds over 5 minutes, also noting the peak value at any point

during the 5 minutes. From the 20 readings at 15-second intervals, calculate a mean value.

The second procedure is necessary as roadside CO levels fluctuate rapidly as traffic passes. Peaks are normally associated with stationary or slow-moving vehicles close to the sampling point. Figure 6.6 shows two typical CO records with readings taken every 15 seconds over 5 minutes. Ideally, a longer sampling period would give a more reliable mean but this may not be practical if you have several sites to sample. Some designs of

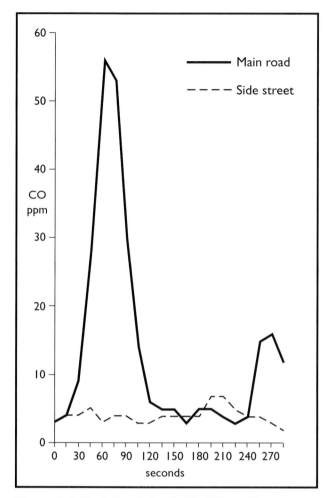

Figure 6.6   Variation in kerbside CO readings.

CO meter can be linked to data loggers enabling continuous monitoring to be carried out, though this might be constrained by the difficulty of finding secure roadside locations where an instrument could be left unattended.

A further use of the CO meter is to carry out transects with spot measurements being taken at fixed intervals (e.g. every 100 metres). This could be done on foot or, for greater distances, experienced cyclists might consider carefully securing the meter to the front of a bicycle. For safety reasons it is important to pull off the road and stop at each sampling point. When interpreting the data, assuming you have only one CO meter, it is important to remember that the readings from different positions on the transect will not be contemporaneous – that is, they will not all have been taken at the same time. Some of the variation may be due to changing weather conditions (such as windspeed) during the sampling period.

As with most pollutants from traffic, you will normally find a reduction in concentration away from roadside sites. CO normally decreases quite sharply away from the roadside due to its

instability in the atmosphere and its tendency to be oxidised to CO_2. It therefore ceases to be a health hazard but, once oxidised, makes its contribution to the greenhouse effect.

Sampling particulates

A great deal can be achieved in investigating air quality and its effects without resorting to expensive equipment. While there are limitations to the qualitative assessment of air pollution itself, several methods are available for assessing the effects of air pollution on plants, buildings and people. Although these are very simple techniques, if carried out carefully they can provide useful qualitative data on spatial variations in one aspect of air quality. Results of such investigations can be supplemented with secondary data about air pollution.

One approach is to expose sample surfaces that have been coated with sticky substances to which airborne particles will adhere. A number of different designs of samplers have been used including plastic petri dishes or microscope slides coated with a thin film of Vaseline. You will need to think carefully about mounting the samplers so that they are secure, as well as standardising the positioning of the samplers. Locate them at a standard height above ground level with the treated surface mounted either face up or vertically. If vertically mounted you will need to think about standardising the orientation, e.g. facing into the wind or towards traffic or with a standard compass direction.

You may need to carry out a pilot study before your main survey to find out what sort of time-period you need to expose samplers for in order to obtain significant deposition. In urban streets six hours should be sufficient. It is better to avoid wet weather as rain will wash particles off, and on dry, windy days you are more likely to catch larger particulate matter blown up from the ground as well as the fine particulates from emissions. After a standard period of exposure samplers are then collected in and compared. You will need to cover the samplers once they have been collected and avoid disturbing the sample surface. Petri dishes can be covered in clingfilm while microscope slides can be slotted into a slide box which keeps slides separate. Analysis can be done by placing the samplers side by side in rank order – that is, with the cleanest at one end of the row and the dirtiest at the other end. If the samplers are of clear plastic you could place each one on a grid or graph paper and use a microscope to count the number of particles deposited per cm². There is ample scope for developing and improving this technique through experimentation.

An alternative approach is to sample particulates from surfaces in the street which have been gathering grime over long periods of time. A simple sampling technique involves using a filter paper as a swab to clean particles off grimy surfaces. A small-diameter filter paper is soaked in methylated spirits then wiped over the surface of a standard area to clean off all the deposited grime. This is then placed in a sealed polythene envelope, carefully labelled for later analysis. If you use this technique to investigate spatial variations in air quality there are a number of site standardisations to consider if comparisons are to be made between them. Reasonably smooth surfaces such as painted metal structures are ideal. Very smooth surfaces such as the front side of roadsigns tend to get washed clean by rainfall. The surfaces must have been exposed to the atmosphere for a similar time period. A sample from a newly erected road sign, for example, would not be comparable to a sample from a long-established lamp-post elsewhere. Furthermore, flat surfaces are easier to sample than curved surfaces. Height above ground level and proximity to passing traffic are important factors to consider. If the sampling surfaces are too close to traffic or to the ground then much of the grime will be particles thrown up by rainsplash or road surface spray in wet weather. With these points in mind the following surfaces have been found to give good results.

- Traffic lights – particularly surfaces on the bracket which attaches the lights to the post. Make sure you don't obscure the lights while sampling.

- Road signs. Sample the reverse side as the coated surface of the road sign itself is often too smooth to retain deposits.

- Tree leaves. Freshly emerged leaves in spring will not have had time to accumulate grime. Later in the year swabs taken from leaves of the same tree species at a standard height above ground level are probably the best way of ensuring comparability between sites. Find trees with low branches so that you don't have to climb trees or use ladders. This may involve finding trees in parks or squares. A sample of swabs taken at 2 metres above ground level from even-sized plane tree leaves at different locations in the city in late summer would be ideal.

Analysis of the filter papers after sampling can involve a similar process to that described for the Vaseline plates. Place in rank order on a sheet of paper, label, and glue in place to provide a visual record of your results. Covering with adhesive film will provide a more permanent record.

To give more quantitative results, filter papers can be dried and weighed to the nearest milligram (mg) before sampling, and then dried and reweighed after sampling to record the weight of particles deposited. Comparison of samples between sites can then be made.

The following resources and sources of information may be useful in undertaking air pollution investigations.

Air pollution monitoring services and equipment
Department of Environment, Transport and the Regions (D.E.T.R.)
Air Pollution Information Service:
website: http://www.environment.detr.gov.uk/airq/aqinfo.htm
Freephone: 0800 556677
Ceefax: 410–417
Teletext: 106

Carbon monoxide meter
Bedfont Scientific Ltd
Bedfont House, Holywell Lane, Upchurch, Kent, ME9 7HN Tel: 01634 375614

Passive samplers and analysis service for NO₂ and SO₂
Dr Darius Krochmal
Institute of Inorganic Chemistry and Technology
Dept of Analytical Chemistry
Krakow University of Technology
ul. Warszawska 24, 31-155 Krakow, Poland
e-mail: krochm@chemia.pk.edu.pl

Diffusion tubes for a range of atmospheric pollutants
Analytical Services
AEA Technology
551 Harwell, Oxfordshire,
OX11 ORA

Transport and sustainability – some case studies

Investigating local transport systems – how they are and how they might be – addresses several key areas of Agenda 21. Future transport priorities will be a crucial factor in projections concerning energy use (particularly fossil fuel consumption), climate change, air quality, human health and issues of social justice. Transport is not just an environmental issue. Depending on what priorities are pursued will also determine whether *all* members of society are free to move around safely and affordably without environmental damage or impingeing on other people's rights to a safe and healthy environment.

Transport – the emerging priorities

New ideas about prioritising transport in towns and cities have the potential to revolutionise transport systems. There are different versions of this priority listing but the order of priority in Figure 6.7 is increasingly being applied by many urban authorities and has been informally acknowledged by the Department of Transport as a basis for future city transport planning. It is interesting to consider to what extent these priorities are based on *environmental factors* and how much they are influenced by *human rights and equality issues*. Would an emphasis on one or the other affect the order of priorities or do environmental and human rights objectives coincide?

A key report which could become a blueprint for sustainable transport has already been drawn up by the Royal Commission on Environmental Pollution. In their eighteenth report, which focuses on transport and the environment, the recommendations specify a list of objectives which, if implemented, would embody much of the spirit of Agenda 21. It is well worth getting hold of

---

Urban transport priorities – a recently proposed ranking
(from various sources)

1. Disabled/elderly
2. Pedestrian
3. Bicycle
4. Bus/Tram/Rail
5. Delivery vehicle
6. Motorcycle
7. Taxi
8. Private car

Figure 6.7 Urban transport priorities.

---

a copy as the specific targets which follow each objective could provide a useful focus for redesigning your local transport systems. Do be aware that Royal Commission reports such as this are *recommendations* to government and they don't necessarily become policy.

Assessing the sustainability of transport systems – a case study of shopping journeys

Recording traffic flows represents a time-honoured fieldwork activity which geographers have been undertaking for years though not always perhaps with a clear vision of why they were doing it. The following example describes methods for investigating the sustainability implications of different types of retailing activity in relation to the fuel used and CO_2 emitted during shopping journeys. The methods show how you might try to quantify the energy used and CO_2 generated by journeys to and from different types of shopping facilities. Some preliminary results for a village store, an inner city high street and an out-of-town superstore are presented.

To obtain these sorts of results you will need to find out the following information.

a) *The fuel (or fuel equivalent) per person per kilometre for each of the methods of transport.* The values quoted in Table 6.5 are derived from a number of sources and should be regarded as approximations. There are many factors which can produce variation above or below these values, particularly vehicle speed, frequency of stopping and starting, vehicle weight, engine size and the precise number of passengers on board. The values quoted are expressed as the amount of fuel and CO_2 generated in transporting one person one kilometre by each method of transport. Clearly, a bus or train won't travel as far as a car on a litre of fuel but this is more than offset by the greater number of passengers normally carried. Pedestrians and cyclists obviously don't drink petrol to move so the fuel amounts quoted are the fuel equivalents of the food energy required to travel 1 km.

b) *A comparable set of data for CO_2 emissions per person per kilometre associated with each method of transport.* (Table 6.5) It could be argued that cyclists will generate a little more CO_2 than a sedentary person in a bus or a car but the difference is negligible relative to the emissions from motorised transport. Electric trains are not emitting CO_2 directly but CO_2 will have normally been released in the power-generating process.

Table 6.5   Fuel use and CO$_2$ emissions for different types of transport

Type of transport	Fuel (l) / person / km*	CO$_2$ (kg) / person / km
Car (driver only)	0.095	0.24
Motorcycle	0.079	0.20
Car (4 passengers)	0.024	0.06
Bus (25 passengers)	0.016	0.05
Underground	0.023	0.05
Pedestrian	0.007	v.small
Bus (70 passengers)	0.006	0.02
Suburban train (250 passengers)	0.005	0.01
Cyclist	0.002	v.small

* for human-powered transport the fuel equivalent of the food energy is quoted.

c) *For a sample of shoppers you will need to find out the method of transport used to travel to the shopping facility and the distance travelled.* This sort of information is quickly gathered using a short questionnaire, provided you approach people in an appropriate manner, but difficulties can arise within the vicinity of superstores as you are likely to be on private property. You would need to approach the store manager and explain what you are doing but be prepared to accept a refusal. Some managers may be reluctant to allow you to carry out such a survey if they feel you may be inconveniencing and therefore discouraging customers or because they are concerned that the information you are gathering could be used in ways that are contrary to the commercial interests of their company. As with any fieldwork but especially if you are approaching members of the public, don't go alone, and discuss your plans with your parents or teacher.

If you are anxious about carrying out this sort of survey then an alternative is to question a sample of your relatives and friends to obtain comparable information, but this sample is less likely to be a representative one.

The calculation steps are as follows:

i)   To determine fuel use multiply the distance travelled in km (this must include outward and return journeys) for each respondent by the fuel use per km for their particular form of transport.

ii) To determine CO$_2$ emission multiply the distance travelled by the CO$_2$ per km value.

If you have a standard sample size (say 100 shoppers) then the totals will be more or less comparable for different facilities.

Figures 6.8 and 6.9 show some tentative results collected by students for a superstore, an inner city high street and a village store. Not surprisingly, superstore users are making much longer journeys than customers of the village store. High street shoppers showed intermediate journey length but the greatest use of public transport. Evidently the emphasis on private car use for journeys to superstores together with the greater distances travelled results in higher energy use and CO$_2$ emissions for the sample of 100 shoppers than is the case for either the high street or village store. This study did not take account of the frequency of shopping journeys undertaken. It is possible that the greater energy use for trips to the superstore might be at least partly offset by a decreased frequency of trip compared with the frequency of trips to the village store or high street.

Do be aware that this method only takes account of the energy used and pollution generated in people travelling from their homes to the retail outlet where they buy their food. It doesn't take account of energy used in transporting produce from its place of production to where you bought it or energy and resources used in processing and packaging. To do this you would need to trace your avocados back to Guatemala, compute the aviation fuel used to fly them to Heathrow, add on the diesel used to take them up the motorway to the warehouse in Warrington where they were stuffed into little polystyrene trays and covered in clingfilm, then add on more fuel to get them to the shop where you bought them. (I'm not sure that avocados follow precisely this route but many imported products have fascinating but fuel-rapacious journeys.) All we've done here is quantify the resources used and carbon emitted in finally transporting the weary avocado from the place where you bought it to the dinner table.

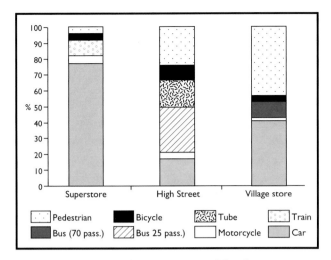

Figure 6.8 Modes of transport used by shoppers.

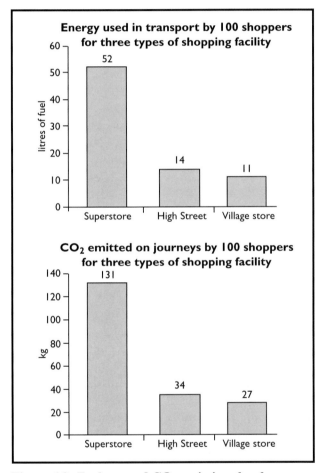

Figure 6.9 Fuel use and CO_2 emissions by shoppers.

Neither have we computed possible emissions of greenhouse gases (such as methane) to the atmosphere after consumption. Though smaller in volume, these could exceed the CO_2 emitted from your car exhaust in terms of their potency as agents of global warming!

Mapping transport space

We are accustomed in urban fieldwork to mapping the uses of buildings but less so to mapping the considerable space between buildings, much of which is used for transportation. Mapping transport space is a useful activity in finding out about present transport priorities and can provide a starting point in re-designing or re-allocating transport space if it is thought desirable. It may also reveal some surprises, such as the amount of urban space between and beneath transport routes which is inaccessible and therefore unused. Liberating such spaces for imaginative uses is an exciting possibility. The spreadsheet printout in Figure 6.10 shows a possible classification suitable for an inner city environment. You may well need to modify this for your local area. Using a large-scale map (preferably the OS 1:1250, the largest scale available for built-up areas) and a colour-coded system, shade in areas according to their transport uses, noting the approximate width of space allocated to each use or mixture of uses.

Then set up a spreadsheet listing all the uses you have identified in your study area. For each use, measure the length and average width for each particular use then in the fourth column add a formula to calculate the area which each use occupies. This can be expressed as a percentage of all transport uses in a further column. You can then draw bar or pie charts to show the space allocation for different transport uses. Figure 6.11 shows the amounts of space devoted to different transport uses for a small area in Hammersmith, west London. In this case, the transport system is three-dimensional as it includes a section of elevated highway, underground train lines and station and an elevated bus station over a shopping precinct. In such cases separate maps for different levels may be necessary.

In the Hammersmith example, the high percentage of main road space reflects the location of the area on main routes out of London and past policies of expanding road space to accommodate growing motor traffic volumes. The small but significant amount of space where cyclists have some priority reflects the beginnings of relatively cycle-friendly borough policies. Which transport types might be given more space and which less space if you wished to move towards a more sustainable transport system?

It would be interesting to undertake a comparative study of places which operate different transport policies. This might take the form of a comparison between a town where the new transport priorities are already affecting policy with one that has pursued more conventional transport policies and not yet adopted new priorities. One of the new

A transport space classification			
(data from worked example in Hammersmith, West London)			
	Length (m)	Average width (m)	Area (m2)
SURFACE SPACE			
Main road - dual carriageway	300.0	20.0	6000.0
Other main road	400.0	10.0	4000.0
Side street(less roadside parking)	430.0	6.0	2580.0
Roadside parking	250.0	2.5	625.0
Off road parking	110.0	90.0	9900.0
Bus lane	45.0	2.5	112.5
Bus lane +taxis and cycles	250.0	2.5	625.0
Cycle lane	240.0	1.0	240.0
Pavement/footpath	2200.0	2.5	5500.0
Pedestrian/cycle crossings	80.0	3.0	240.0
Dead space between/beneath roads	300.0	20.0	6000.0
SUB-SURFACE SPACE			
Underground rail	200.0	50.0	10000.0
Pedestrian subway	150.0	4.0	600.0
ELEVATED SPACE			
Elevated highway	400.0	20.0	8000.0
Bus station	95.0	50.0	4750.0
Total transport related space			59172.5
(all levels)			
	SUMMARY PERCENTAGES OF:		
	Roadway and parking		52.6
	Bus provision		9.3
	Rail		16.9
	Pedestrian		10.5
	Cycle lane		0.6
	Dead space		10.1

Figure 6.10 Transport space classification.

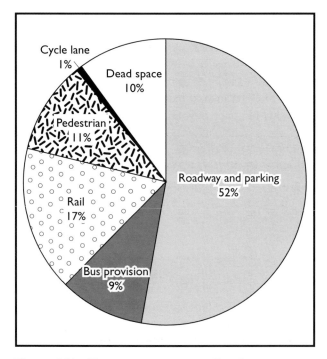

Figure 6.11   Transport space, west London.

towns such as Milton Keynes where planning took account of a range of transport users, not just motor vehicles, would be a good example of the former. If the opportunity arises, a comparison between a UK town and one elsewhere, in those parts of Europe where balanced transport policies have become the norm, would be of interest. London with its lack of an integrated transport policy covering the whole urban area provides opportunities for comparisons between boroughs which operate different transport priorities.

A public transport access survey

While public transport obviously uses energy, generates pollution (directly or indirectly) and takes up space, these effects are generally less than for the private car (see Table 6.5). Most scenarios of more sustainable transport systems would therefore envisage a transfer of emphasis from car usage to public transport with a range of direct and indirect benefits arising. The indirect benefits would include reduction in journey times for buses and taxis arising from reduced congestion and more pleasant road conditions which would encourage people to walk and cycle more. There are, though, potential areas of concern in such a shift. The dependency of many forms of public transport on the diesel engine raises the issue of PM10s – tiny particulates emitted from diesel exhausts especially if engines are poorly maintained, and which are increasingly thought to be a health risk.

Remembering that Agenda 21 is about total quality of life, including social justice as well as a healthy and more sustainable environment, it is important that public transport is accessible to all and that it can integrate with other forms of transport.

A survey of public transport access can be undertaken by observation and by making enquiries at public transport facilities in your survey area. It involves considering how accessible each transport facility is to a range of users. An inventory of possible users who might experience problems of access to different public transport facilities is listed in the rows of a matrix, with categories of transportation forming the columns (Figure 6.12). Cells can then be filled in with an assessment of the ease of accessibility for each category of user. In most situations an assessment could be made on the basis of imagining the needs of each category of user and comparing these with the access provided. Such a survey can be used to identify the combinations of user and transport type where people in particular circumstances will be excluded or denied access. Recognising such constraints then provides a springboard for change.

Cycling options

It has been suggested that one of the cheapest and quickest ways to move towards more sustainable urban transport systems is to increase the proportion of journeys undertaken by cycle and on foot. In relation to cycling, one of the targets in the

Circumstances of user	Local train/ tram	Underground train	Inter city train	Local bus *	Long distance coach	Taxi	Mini-cab
Disabled - wheelchair with helper							
Disabled - independent with wheelchair							
Disabled - blind							
Person with young children and pushchair							
Cyclist with conventional cycle							
Cyclist with folding bike							
* The situation may vary according to the design/size of vehicle							

Figure 6.12   Public transport access survey.

Royal Commission report on Transport and the Environment (amidst a total of 110 recommendations! – see Figure 6.13 for a summary) is:

> *To increase cycle use to 10% of all urban journeys by 2005, compared to 2.5% now, and seek further increases thereafter . . .*

This proposal in the Royal Commission report has now been incorporated into government policy as part of the National Cycling Strategy (CTC/IHT, 1996).

This is a modest objective, especially in the light of the much higher proportions of cycle journeys already undertaken by some of our European neighbours. Let's consider some of the options that could be applied to your local area if you wished to increase the proportion of cycle journeys.

There are a range of different approaches proposed by different individuals among cycle campaigners and transport planners. Some favour the more obvious strategy of creating segregated cycle lanes which increase the safety and comfort of cyclists, thereby encouraging greater cycle use. Others see such strategies as marginalising cyclists which could lead to their exclusion from direct main routes. They would claim that cycling policies should focus on restricting or discouraging vehicle use (traffic reduction) to allow bikes to become a more dominant form of transport on the existing mixed-use road network. If you cycle in urban

---

Extracts from the eighteenth report of the Royal Commission on Environmental Pollution on 'Transport and the Environment' (1994)

Some of the key objectives

Objective A
To ensure that an effective transport policy at all levels of government is integrated with land use policy and gives priority to minimising the need for transport and increasing the proportion of trips made by environmentally less damaging modes.

Objective B
To achieve standards of air quality that will prevent damage to human health and the environment.

Objective C
To improve the quality of life, particularly in towns and cities, by reducing the dominance of cars and lorries and providing alternative means of access.

Objective F
To reduce carbon dioxide emissions from transport.

Objective G
To reduce substantially the demands which transport infrastructure and the vehicle industry place on non-renewable materials.

For some of these objectives, targets are set to determine when the objectives should be met.

Figure 6.13   'Transport and the Environment' objectives.

areas yourself you will no doubt have your own views on such matters. Before considering what cycling strategies you would recommend it might be worth finding out from cyclists how they perceive their needs. Several cities now have cycling pressure groups who campaign for a more cycle-friendly environment. Figure 6.14 suggests some of the measures that have been attempted to improve conditions for cyclists in towns. Not all of these necessarily meet with the approval of all cyclists or indeed other road users. Many campaigners for cyclists' rights favour making the whole road network safe for cyclists through policies such as traffic reduction measures rather than simply by creating segregated cycle lanes.

Cycle hazard mapping

A useful focus for designing a cycle-friendly environment would be to consider routes to and from school. Start by mapping hazards along particular routes between home and school. Hazards and discomforts commonly experienced by urban cyclists might include the following.

- Main roads with fast-moving traffic, especially where slip-roads join and leave.
- Heavily congested streets, especially with multiple lanes of traffic.
- Right turns in heavy traffic which involve pulling out to the centre of the road.
- Left-hand filter lanes which require cyclists going straight on to pull out into the centre or right-hand lane (any manoeuvre that involves changing lanes with heavy or fast traffic approaching from the rear creates a hazard).
- Roundabouts, especially with multiple lanes.
- Minor routes crossing main roads without traffic lights.
- Traffic-light-controlled crossings over wide main roads with limited time-lapse between phases.

Examples of facilities for improving urban cycling

1. **Cycle lanes**
There are several variations of these. Some are segregated lanes separated from other traffic by physical barriers. Others involve road markings which segregate a metre-wide lane at the edge of the road. Some of these are of an advisory nature only and are popular parking places for some motorists. (Attempts to design cycle lanes around roundabouts tend to create complexity and confusion and are not generally regarded as helpful in reducing danger.)

2. **Shared routes with pedestrians through parks, along towpaths and old railway tracks**
Their safe use requires care, especially on the part of cyclists. There are many places where cyclists and pedestrians co-exist safely, though often cyclists are officially not permitted on such routes. Busy routes may require segregation of cyclists and pedestrians by a white line.

3. **Contra-flow cycle lanes**
This is a special form of segregated cycle lane which allows cyclists to travel the 'wrong way' down one-way streets. Generally, one-way streets are perceived as an inconvenience by cyclists, causing long detours.

4. **Traffic-light-controlled cycle crossings where cycle routes cross or join main roads**
Traffic lights are equipped with a phase specifically for cyclists and sometimes pedestrians.

5. **Advance stop lines**
These are stop lines for cyclists at traffic lights positioned in advance of the vehicle stop line. They allow cyclists to get away in advance of motor vehicles and prevent cyclists from having to queue close to vehicle exhausts.

6. **Cycle parking rails**
The frequency of urban cycle theft has been identified as one of the factors that discourages some people from cycling in towns. The provision of cycle parking rails, or even more secure cycle lockers, at popular locations (especially at railway, bus and underground stations) is one way of encouraging cycle use and helping to integrate cycling with public transport.

Figure 6.14 Facilities for improving urban cycling.

Some traffic-calming measures such as speed humps and chicanes which have been introduced partly with the intention of encouraging cycling have created new hazards and discomforts for cyclists.

The next step is to design new routes which either avoid these hazards without major increases in distance travelled, or, where this is not possible, to create provisions which remove, diminish or avoid the hazard. An excellent reference manual is now available which provides ideas for cycle-friendly designs and layouts (CTC/IHT, 1996).

A further possibility for cycle route studies would be to see how local routes might link into the emerging 5,000-mile national long-distance cycle network, a project being promoted by SUSTRANS. This will be a network for both long-distance and local journeys for recreational and commuting purposes designed for pedestrians, disabled people and cyclists.

How far do you go?

A further dimension to envisaging more sustainable transport systems comes from focusing on where things are in the city rather than the transport system in isolation. There are a whole range of policies which could simply decrease the need for journeys thereby alleviating many of the problems which a city with high levels of mobility gives rise to. Much is talked of the economies of scale which are supposed to result from having a few large facilities such as hospitals, superstores and schools rather than more numerous, closely spaced smaller facilities. These conventional economies may prove to be an illusion once the added environmental and social costs resulting from longer journeys to more centralised facilities are taken into account.

A useful piece of field investigation could involve studies of the distance that individuals travel to buy a range of commodities or to make use of a range of services. The following list could be used to find out how many basic goods and services are still available in the immediate vicinity of people's homes and how many require longer journeys to centralised facilities:

Hardware goods (ironmongery, tools, etc.)
Building and plumbing supplies
Carpets and furnishings
Meat

Bread
Cinema
Accident and emergency facilities

Through interviews, a historical perspective could be introduced by asking older people where they used to go to obtain various goods and services compared with present-day locations. Maps showing desire lines can then be drawn up to see if there has been any change in journey lengths.

Participating in change

Having investigated an issue such as air quality, local transport, or the use of urban land, we may conclude that all is well and existing practice poses no threat to ecosystems far or near, to other communities or to future generations, and there are no infringements of anyone's human rights. If this is the case we can write up our investigation, hand it in for assessment and breathe a sigh of relief. What do we do, though, if on applying indicators of sustainability to the current situation we find that all is not well? What if our investigations reveal unacceptable levels of pollution in air or water? What if we find systems of production, consumption and transportation which use and waste scarce resources? What if we find plans for developments which will violate the landscape and reduce biodiversity? What if we reveal economic and political systems which deny people their basic rights? Should we attempt to change things and, if so, how?

The process of trying to bring about change for a better world as a result of what we have discovered can be seen as an integral part of geographical fieldwork. Some of the strategies for fieldwork examined in earlier chapters highlight personal decision-making and action as the culmination of the process of geographical enquiry (see Figures 3.7 and 3.8 in Chapter 3). How we go about promoting change involves a very careful consideration of both our values in relation to the various environmental perspectives (see Chapter 2) and our political inclinations. There are many ways of influencing change – through our choices in what we buy and consume (or refrain from buying or consuming), what lifestyle we adopt, through seeking to influence decision-makers in governments and commerce, through participating in actions against what we see as unacceptable, or through setting up with others different ways of doing and living which offer tangible alternatives to established practice. Table 6.6 attempts to summarise four different systems of decision-making in relation to ecological concerns, each of which is to some extent associated with both a particular ecological view and a particular political stance.

Both globally and in the UK, recent years have seen a shift towards the free market process with a noticeable emphasis towards decisions affecting the environment being taken by those in power in the industrial and commercial world. The effect of privatisation and de-regulation means that many decisions which relate to the sustainability of ecosystems and human communities are now taken by people in the commercial world rather than by people in central or local government or by communities themselves. Most decisions concerning transport, water resources, and energy, for example, are now increasingly in the hands of industrialists and business people, though with variable degrees of influence from government-controlled regulating authorities. If you wished to bring about change through the operation of the free market you would need to put pressure on companies to try and influence their policies and practices. Environmental campaigning frequently involves seeking to effect change through all four channels. Presenting your arguments clearly and forcefully to corporations as well as to central and local government departments is often an initial stage in mounting campaigns to oppose damaging developments or promote better policies. If such endeavours fail to achieve the desired result, then you may wish to consider, with others, the appropriateness of more direct forms of action.

The option of becoming involved in non-violent direct action campaigns may seem daunting, especially as such campaigns are frequently misrepresented by the media who often try to portray participants as anti-social and threatening. Meeting and talking with participants involved in such campaigns may reveal a different picture. Non-violent direct action (NVDA) has a long and noble tradition and includes such revered people as Mahatma Ghandi, the many peace campaigners of the post-war years and the commitment of road protesters and land rights ecologists of more recent times. The results of direct action campaigning may not always be immediately obvious or tangible. Recent campaigns against the construction of new roads, for example, may not have succeeded in halting specific schemes but

they achieved a range of outcomes which will affect future road-building schemes as well as bringing issues surrounding road construction to wider public attention.

Suggestions for further activities

- After discussion with others in a small group, try to reach a definition of sustainability that you can all agree upon. To focus discussion, try concentrating on the relative importance of:
  time-spans
  resource use
  attitude to nature
  social equity
  self-reliance.

- Using your definition of sustainability, put forward five key indicators of sustainability that could be applied to your locality.

- Find out how the following activities function in terms of use of resources, distance over which goods are transported, self-reliance of users and participants, and management of waste products:
  a supermarket
  a local allotment
  a fast-food outlet.
  Then apply your five key indicators of sustainability.

- Try out some of the stimulus activities in Figure 6.1 then use the experiences to identify three aspects of your local environment which could provide opportunities for fieldwork investigations with a sustainability flavour.

- Consider the four means of implementing environmental change in Table 6.6. What are the opportunities and limitations of each in achieving change towards more sustainable objectives? Which means of implementing change is best suited to achieving more sustainable ways of living?

- What environmental issue in your locality is most relevant to ideas concerning a more sustainable world? What might you do to investigate it further? What might you do to bring about changes in policies and practice in relation to this issue?

Table 6.6   Viewpoints on environmental policy and implementing change

Free market capitalism	Government regulation of the free market	Democratic control of local economies	Radical green community action
The free market in conjunction with science and technology will solve resource shortages and pollution problems.	Regulation of the free market by central government (laws, planning and taxation) to achieve environmental protection.	Local government exercises strict controls on capitalism to limit harmful impacts.	Envisages a radical change to the present order to achieve a vision of sustainable living and social equity.
'Business as usual'.	Economic growth necessary to alleviate poverty and to solve environmental problems by technical means.	Mix of common and private ownership.	People organise themselves in order to have responsibility and control over their own lives.
Economic growth (measured by GNP) essential for meeting rising material expectations.	Parliamentary democracy can regulate the operation of the market to ensure that it takes account of environmental costs.	Low growth favoured or measures of growth which include quality of life.	Change to be brought about by direct action. This may take the form of action (e.g. road protests) to try and prevent what are perceived as destructive policies, or the setting up of alternative uses of space (e.g. land occupations for ecological purposes, 'critical mass' cyclists' actions).
The environment is viewed as being important for maintaining the supply of resources necessary for growth.	Democratically-elected central government includes regulatory authorities which oversee the activities of large corporations.	Aim to achieve greater equity and environmental improvement through local regulation.	
If resources get scarce, substitutes will be found.		State subsidy of public services (e.g. public transport).	Present problems are viewed as part of an environmental crisis which could be solved by creating self-reliant communities.
Consumer pressure will cause businesses to act in the interests of the environment.		Favour appropriate technology.	
Directors of business and industry have greatest power but respond to consumer pressure through the market.		Power rests with local government responding to local priorities.	Pressure on resources reduced by adoption of simpler lifestyles.
			No power structure is involved as decisions are reached by consensus at community level.

Conclusion

The new directions in geographical fieldwork outlined in this book have been concerned both with *what* we focus on as themes for worthwhile investigation in geographical fieldwork and *how* we might go about such investigations.

The *how* is all about methods, planning and approaches. If you have persevered this far (unless you've flipped straight to the Conclusion!), you may be aware of some imbalance in those sections dealing with methods. Several sections have discussed the limitations of an overemphasis on quantitative approaches, arguing that recent advances in geographical thinking are better suited to methods that rely on description and allow scope for feelings and individual interpretations to be expressed. The case studies, however, tend to begin with qualitative experiences which lead into key questions which are then often answered using quantitative approaches.

I may rightly be accused of failing to 'put my money where my mouth is'. There are two related reasons though for this apparent discrepancy. Firstly, there are currently very few examples of recent geographical project work at school level which rely wholly on qualitative approaches. The quantitative approaches adopted in the 1960s remain dominant and this is reflected in much (but not all) of the guidance currently offered by exam boards where there is an optional or compulsory field-based project forming a component of the examination. This situation is likely to change as exam boards begin to acknowledge the acceptability of the qualitative approaches which are now commonplace in academic geography.

There can also be a kind of inbuilt inertia in fieldwork which arises when students are advised to look through past titles in arriving at a project topic. The result of such a process is that both methods and topics are continually recycled, stifling originality and failing to incorporate either the new priorities of a rapidly changing world or new ideas in geography.

It is possible that by adopting some of the approaches in this book you may experience a critical response to your ideas. Projects based on qualitative methods may be criticised for being 'woolly', 'vague' or 'unscientific'. Themes that challenge established power structures may be derided for being too 'political', 'subversive' or 'radical'. Be prepared to support your proposals, perhaps by referring to some of the ideas about methods developed in Chapter 3, or the arguments for incorporating a sustainability emphasis developed in Chapter 6. If, though, you are advised against a certain proposal because it is too hazardous then it would be sensible to think again.

We might summarise the evolving approaches to fieldwork in geography over past decades as having moved from a concern with somewhat uncritical descriptions and syntheses of landscapes to an interest in explanation, a trend which tended to lead us away from embracing the whole scene towards a focus on parts, and from descriptive methods to quantitative methods. The subsequent trend led us towards the sort of fieldwork which critically assessed the relationship between people and the environment. An exciting opportunity for further development of this theme is to go beyond such critical evaluations of human activity in relation to the Earth towards field-based activities which can contribute to an era of human presence on the Earth which respects rather than degrades nature, spreads beauty rather than ugliness and unites rather than divides.

For many geographers – old and young – fieldwork is associated with new and lasting insights, memories of fine landscapes and companionship, explorations in new environments, perhaps moments of intense emotion arising from an encounter with the natural world and revelations of deeper meanings. To these traditional attributes we might add the potential of field experiences to act as springboards for debating and enacting change towards a better world. Such intentions are likely to arise as much from our emotional responses to places as to our careful recordings and measurements. At the start of this book a student's experience was quoted in which she felt that anger was an inappropriate response in geographical fieldwork. We are now beginning to move away from the idea of the geographer merely as a detached observer, towards the recognition of a geographer as primarily an ordinary person with the usual range of emotions, but equipped with certain perceptions and skills which encourage sensitivity not only to beauty and harmony but also to instances of injustice or despoilment in our surroundings. To strengthen such perceptions, our recent reliance on the dominance of scientific explanations of our surroundings might be tempered by placing greater trust in our feelings and senses; and added to our concern with explaining things as they are, we may also need to develop our critical and imaginative faculties to envision how they might be in the future.

Bibliography

Barnett, M., Kent, A. and Mitten, M. (editors) (1995) *Images of Earth – a teachers' guide to remote sensing in geography at Key Stage 3 and GCSE*, The Geographical Association.

Brough, E. (1983) 'Geography through art' in J. Huckle (ed.) *Geography Education: reflection and action*, Oxford University Press, Oxford.

Chorley, R. (1970) 'The role and relations of physical geography' in *Progress in Geography*, 3, 87–109.

Cyclists Touring Club/Institute of Highways and Transportation (1996) *Cycle-friendly Infrastructure: Guidelines for Planning and Design*, CTC/IHT in association with the Bicycle Association and the Department of Transport.

Department of Transport (1996) *National Cycling Strategy*, Department of Transport, DITM Division, Great Minster House, 76 Marsham Street, London SW1P 4DR.

Devall, B. and Sessions, G. (1985) *Deep Ecology – living as if nature mattered*, Gibbs Smith, Salt Lake City, USA.

Eckersley, R. (1992) *Environmentalism and Political Theory: towards an ecocentric approach*, UCL Press, London.

Everson, J.A. (1973) 'Fieldwork in school geography' in R. Walford *New Directions in Geography Teaching*, Longman, London.

Frew, J. (1993) *Advanced Geography Fieldwork*, Nelson, London.

Gleick, J. (1987) *Chaos*, Heinemann.

Goudie, A. (1994) 'The Nature of Physical Geography: A view from the drylands', *Geography* 79 (3), 194–209.

Hails, J.R. (1975) 'Sediment distribution and Quaternary history of Start Bay', *Jl. Geol. Soc.*, London, 131, 63–68.

Harvey, P.K. (1991) *The Role and Value of A-level Geography Fieldwork: A Case Study*. Unpublished PhD thesis, University of Durham.

Hawkins, G. (1987) 'From awareness to participation: New directions in the outdoor experience', *Geography* 72 (1), 217–222.

Hesse, H. (1920) *Wandering*, translated edition 1988, Triad/Paladin, London.

Hutchings, G. (1955) *An Introduction to Geographical Landscape Drawing*, reprinted 1983, Field Studies Council, Occasional Publication No. 5.

Job, D.A. (1988) 'Changes in village services – the use of trade directories', *Geography Review* 2 (2), 11–13.

Job, D.A. (1989) 'Beach profiles and wave action', *Geography Review* 2 (3), 11–14.

Job, D.A. (1993a) 'The Start Bay barrier beach system', in Burt T.P. (ed.) *A Field Guide to the Geomorphology of the Slapton Region*, BGRG/FSC, Occasional publication.

Job, D.A. (1993b) 'Start Bay, South Devon – coastal management past and present', *Geography Review* 7 (2), 13–17.

Job, D.A. (1994a) 'Investigating air quality', *Geography Review* 7 (3), 33–37.

Job, D.A. (1994b) 'New approaches to studying retail locations', *Geography Review* 7 (5), 25–29.

Job, D.A. (1995a) 'Geography with attitude', *Geography Review* 8 (4), 33–37.

Job, D.A. (1995b) 'Projects towards sustainability – 1. Local transport fieldwork', *Geography Review* 9 (1), 25–30.

Job, D.A. and Slater, F. (1996) *Schools Network on Air Pollution: Report of Findings 1995*, Institute of Education, University of London.

Kirby, C. (1995) 'Urban Air Pollution', *Geography* 80 (4) No. 349.

Lenon, B. and Cleves, P. (1994) *Fieldwork Techniques and Projects in Geography*, Collins Educational, London.

Lovelock, J. (1979) *Gaia – a New Look at Life on Earth*, Oxford University Press, Oxford.

McDonagh, S. (1986) To care for the Earth: A call to a new theology, Geoffrey Chapman, London.

Naish, M., Rawling, E. and Hart, C. (1987) *Geography 16–19 The contribution of a curriculum project to 16–19 education*, Longman.

Pethick, J. (1984) *An Introduction to Coastal Geomorphology*, Edward Arnold.

Read, C. (ed.) (1994) *How Vehicle Pollution Affects our Health*, Ashden Trust, 9 Red Lion Court, London EC4A 3EB.

Robinson, A.H.W. (1961) 'The hydrography of Start Bay and its relationship to beach changes at Hallsands', *Geographical Journal* 127, 63–77.

Royal Commission on Environmental Pollution (1994) *Eighteenth Report: Transport and the Environment*, HMSO, London.

Thomas, R.S. (1993) *Collected Poems 1945–1990*, Dent, London.

Wooldridge, S.W. and East, W.G. (1951) *The Spirit and Purpose of Geography*, Hutchinson, London.

Worth, R.H. (1904, 1909, 1923) 'Hallsands and Start Bay', *Trans. Devon Assoc.* 36, 302–46; 41, 301–8; 55, 131–47.

Index

Note: **bold** page numbers indicate
glossary definitions